MANY HANDS
MANY MIRACLES

by
FATHER DAN MADIGAN
and
ANN BANCROFT

photographs by
DAVE BROOKS
BILL GOIDELL

University of Notre Dame Press
Notre Dame, Indiana 46556

YAP 5/7/97

COPYRIGHT 1996 BY
UNIVERSITY OF NOTRE DAME PRESS
NOTRE DAME, INDIANA 46556
ALL RIGHTS RESERVED

Manufactured in the United States of America

DESIGN BY MARTINEZ/HARDY DESIGN & COMMUNICATION

LIBRARY OF CONGRESS CATALOGING-IN-PUBLICATION DATA
A CIP catalog record for this book is available from the
Library of Congress upon request.

ISBN 0-268-01426-4

Father Dan Madigan and Ann Bancroft

ACKNOWLEDGMENTS

As the title of this book indicates, every part of Sacramento Food Bank Services is enriched by the participation of many individuals. This book is no exception. We especially want to thank several people who, though previously unconnected with SFBS, believed in this project enough to donate their time and talents toward its completion. Robin Hardy and Craig Martinez, of the award-winning Martinez/Hardy Design & Communications, donated many hours creating the graphics and arranging for the photographs in the book. Two wonderful photographers, Dave Brooks and Bill Goidell, worked lovingly with clients to give visual life to the services SFBS provides and the people it serves. Both beautifully captured the feeling of clients and programs – Dave, through studio portraits and Bill through documentary photography.

Jennifer Kaufman and Jane Gross, two of the busiest women we know, nevertheless found time for meticulous copy editing and consistent encouragement.

SFBS clients themselves gave openly of their stories, sharing painful memories, revealing difficult lives. Each one of the agency's dedicated staff helped in smoothing the way for interviews with clients, and offered hours for interviews with themselves. From the inception of this project to its completion, SFBS General Manager Jay Schenirer helped keep us on track, organized and inspired. We are grateful for his patience and persistence. SFBS is blessed with a generous and devoted advisory board, whose members have given unwavering support to Father Dan and all his programs. Truly the backbone of the operation, they each deserve mention: Chairman Charles Sylva, Thomas Aguer, Diane Banchero, James Diepenbrock, Bill Garrison, Leighton Hatch, Archie Milligan, Archibald Mull III, Beverly Rosinski, Ilham Saca, Randall Schaber, Paul Taylor, Fred Teichert and Tina Thomas.

Friends and family who deserve thanks for their loving encouragement along the way include Leslie Elgood, Eileen Elfsten, Spring Rodman, Kathie Smith, Lucy Bancroft, Irwin Karp, Matt Moore, Sean Witt and Martine Schoordijk-Tabilio.

For the many miracles, we thank God.

FOREWORD

THE STORY OF SACRAMENTO FOOD BANK SERVICES is really hundreds of stories of real people struggling with human imperfection. It is a story of those who reach out to others in the hope that from brokenness will come wholeness and from dispirited rejection will come a belief in the worth of being. It is about second chances, where those in need are renewed through the helping hands of caring people.

Sacramento Food Bank Services is a collection of diverse talents, abilities and resources focused on one thing: rebuilding the human spirit. It is an organization comprised of teachers, warehouse workers, dentists, lawyers, college students, truck drivers – the spectrum of faces from throughout this region. The efforts of contributors who volunteer time and talent revitalize both those who give and those who receive. In this work Sacramento Food Bank Services contributes to the wholeness and well-being of the Sacramento community. Through uniting the haves and the have-nots, the programs of SFBS build a deeper understanding of human experience in the community. They contribute tangible items – food, clothing, shelter – which improve the quality of life in Sacramento. More importantly, they contribute unseen consequential items – from the recognition that individuals can make a difference, to training that enables recipients to grab hold of their lives and make them count. Both the tangible items and the development of personal attitudes which produce constructive actions contribute mightily to Sacramento.

This entire program, which now provides goods and services valued at around $10 million a year, springs from the simple vision of an unassuming man. Fr. Dan Madigan grew up in Ireland, the son of parents who believed Providence sent the poor to their door so they could help them. After being ordained and coming to the Sacramento Diocese, Fr. Dan was first assigned to a poor parish. He then went to an affluent church but asked to be reassigned as pastor to an inner-city neighborhood. This experience put him in a unique position through which he could link the human desire for fulfillment with the concrete needs of the poor. A shy man by nature, Fr. Dan, acting as an advocate for those in need, became very adept at recruiting volunteers and raising funds.

Joe Serna, Jr., a political activist who later became mayor of Sacramento, frequently stopped by the first Sacramento Food Bank facility. He tells the story of how in its early years Sacramento Food Bank Services raised some modest funds by selling large pretzels. The pretzels cost 50 cents. Joe says he normally would drop 50 cents in a canister each time he visited, without taking a pretzel. One day Fr. Dan approached him at the pretzel canister.

"Joe, I've been meaning to talk to you," Fr. Dan said.

"Yeah, Father, you're probably wondering why I drop 50 cents in the canister and never take a pretzel. I don't really like pretzels," Joe explained.

"No, no. What I really wanted to tell you was, – well, a week ago the pretzels went to 75 cents."

Through active fund raising and spirited community involvement, Sacramento Food Bank Services grew. The way in which it grew and fulfilled human need is a model for other communities. By recognizing the God-given desire to be more than just our insular selves, SFBS attracted volunteers, which translated into time, energy and money. The everyday needs of sustenance – food, shelter, clothing – were provided through programs which met the reciprocal needs of both givers and recipients. With his straightforward vision, Fr. Madigan became a catalyst for the formation of what is now an organization with multiple programs. His links with two separate worlds existing in the same community made it possible. Most American cities house separate worlds of poverty and affluence. Linking these worlds through contacts with each can unleash tremendous energy for good.

In meeting immediate needs, Sacramento Food Bank Services performs simple acts which deal with some of the elements of poverty. True poverty, however, is not merely a lack of things. Hopelessness, helplessness and lack of values are characteristics that rob humans of their sense of worth. Without a belief in our ability to make a difference, we all suffer the worst poverty of all – poverty of the spirit.

Unfortunately, many of the programs seeking to help those with little or no material means stress only the tangible handouts. Absent is any effort to deal with the issues of values, or lack of them. This is the real travesty of so many bureaucratic programs. It is only programs like those of Sacramento Food Bank Services, which focus on the whole person – giving training and encouragement along with handouts – that possess any chance at providing meaningful help.

This book is a description of how a program staffed by people who care can accomplish something neither government bureaucracy nor institutional mandate can – reconstruction of a human spirit. There are failures and there are mere holding patterns, but above the loss and the struggle, there is a realization that those who give of their time and energy can rekindle hope. In many ways, this is the story of the Sacramento "Hope" Bank.

David Allen

Rafael Torres accompanies mom to Mother-Baby workshops

CONTENTS

Introduction

I WAS THE YOUNGEST OF NINE CHILDREN around the table, growing up in a rural area of Ireland. We were neither rich nor poor, but we learned about poverty from Mom, who had seen much of it as a child. In Ireland we had tinkers, as we called them, instead of street people who begged at our door. Only once did I ever see Mom turn anyone away, and I'll never forget her remorse. A tinker knocked when Mom was very busy and rushed for time. She sent him packing abruptly without a morsel. After a few thoughtful moments, out the door she ran, chasing him down the road and calling him back to a hot meal. She always believed that any poor person who knocked at the door was sent by Divine Providence. Who can say she was not right?

At the time of my ordination in 1964, it was customary for the newly ordained to single out a few lines of Scripture, place it on an ordination card and make it one's overall goal for life. The quotation I chose was: "The Spirit of the Lord is Upon me; He has anointed me and sent me to preach the Gospel to the poor, to restore the broken-hearted." Often times since, I have felt that the Lord really took me at my word. For the greater part of the past 30 years He has given me the privilege of a ringside seat among the poor.

Coming from a very limited, rural environment, where even Protestants were foreigners to me, I was sent to a parish in a place whose name I could barely pronounce – Del Paso Heights, Sacramento.

Del Paso Heights was a sprawling, rural slum. Included in the parish was the district of Rio Linda, the down-at-heel community frequently disparaged by Rush Limbaugh. There seemed to be no substance in Del Paso Heights, certainly no charm. Poverty and racial unrest existed, but in those days, so did law and order. People in the neighborhood looked to the church for their social life, and despite the bleak surroundings, it was a busy, happy place.

In 1970, I got "promoted" to the wealthiest parish in the city. It was in a neighborhood Sacramentans call the Fabulous Forties – because its streets are numbered in the forties, its homes are enormous and gardens grand. Ronald Reagan lived there at the time, as governor of California. And, after my cozy days of fellowship and feeling needed among the poor, I was absolutely lost.

Early on, one of the ladies of the parish came in and said, "I'd like you to come by and see me." I said "sure", although I'd only been there about a week. I found her home, in the center of the Fabulous Forties. The lady invited me back to a large and lovely breakfast room, and within minutes, started crying.

"Oh, no," I thought, wondering what terrible problem she must have had. It turned out the woman was crying because she had moved into the neighborhood and found herself in over her head, socially. She wasn't fitting into the tennis club, or something.

I had no clue of what to say. After my days of feeling useful among the poor in Del Paso Heights, I couldn't imagine what God wanted of me there. I decided I may as well go off somewhat on my own. Without asking permission of the church, I enrolled in the master's program at California State University, Sacramento, and pursued my degree in social work. I'm grateful to my family for underwriting the tuition.

Squeezing my required field work around parish responsibilities, I helped organize a union of domestic workers and shared in the establishing of a senior drop-in center for the lonely residents of downtown hotels. In 1976 I applied for a position once again in a

poor neighborhood – Immaculate Conception Church in Oak Park. It was there that I began to work at forging links between the two worlds of affluence and poverty in our city. I learned there was a purpose in my time in the Fabulous Forties. If I had stayed in poverty all the time, I'd never have developed the connections I did.

I am still amazed that impoverished areas and neighborhoods of wealth can exist within such a short distance of each other in a city and still have no interaction.

Oak Park is a neighborhood struggling against poverty, crime and drugs to restore pride in its turn-of-the-century wood frame homes and tree-canopied streets. Banners on street lights proclaim "Oak Park, est. 1889." To anyone familiar with inner-city Chicago, Detroit or Harlem, Oak Park might appear a lovely, working-class area. In fact, there are "worse" neighborhoods in Sacramento, and far "worse" in larger California cities. But 80 percent of Oak Park's 18,000 residents receive some form of government aid, according to *The Sacramento Bee*, and more than half of its children live below the poverty line. One in five Oak Park households is headed by a single parent, and more than a third classify themselves as "non-families."

Because the struggles for survival in neighborhoods like Oak Park are less obvious than those frequently chronicled in big-city slums, they are often ignored. It is easier for those who live comfortably in economically healthy cities like Sacramento to lament the poverty of Chicago's housing projects than it is to drive down on a regular basis to a neighborhood like Oak Park and attempt to tackle such poverty, person-to-person.

In my days as a parish priest in Oak Park, I awoke frequently to gunshots, shooed prostitutes from the church steps and startled drunken homeless men curled up by the dumpster.

Less than a mile away, state workers and professionals live in comfortable, Tudor-style homes in another tree-lined neighborhood. Residents of the two neighborhoods move side by side in their own worlds and yet are worlds apart. Moving on both sides of the fence, I get to see strong families with career aspirations as well as grade school dropouts from crime-infested streets. Over the past 20 years, it has been my objective to bring the two worlds closer together.

Constantly I ask what future have people with zero skills, zero work habits, zero role models and zero aspirations. Is it idleness, illiteracy, irresponsibility and illegitimacy that causes all this? Is it alcoholism, drug abuse, criminality and violence that lead to this destitution? Are burglaries, muggings and rape the chicken or the egg? Is the lack of money the sole cause of poverty? Could a change in economics set everything right?

With the philosophy of "It's better to light a candle than curse the darkness," we began operating a food locker and soup kitchen in Oak Park. It started small, with 250 meals served each week. I asked members of my parish to volunteer, and word spread among parishioners in wealthier areas. There was no money for advertising, so I wrote regular letters to the community, describing the growth of our programs and appealing for help. Several of those letters, written as our programs have grown over the past 20 years, are included in this book.

When we opened a second food locker back in Del Paso Heights in 1983, most of our volunteers came from the wealthy Arden Park neighborhood across the freeway. They'd drive up in their Mercedes' and get down in the trenches. Women with their own maids working at home would daily clean and salvage donated vegetables, and pass them out in bags to the poor.

The food lines grew faster than we could expand our storage in the early years. I soon learned that to meet the growing needs we would have to get sophisticated about fundraising. It was clear that more than hand-outs were needed, and that support of the broader community was essential. If I were to fulfill the goal on my ordination card, I would have to seek help from outside the church.

With the encouragement of loyal friends, I overcame my own shyness and set about building relationships in the local business community. I found there were generous, successful, spiritual people of all faiths who were willing to serve as board members and prominent supporters of our programs. With the firm support of local media and businesses, we built a foundation that enabled us to grow and fulfill our vision of "not just handing out fish, but teaching people how to fish."

We've found that providing the basic needs of food and clothing is only the first step in addressing what is really needed to heal the pain of the chronically poor. Family togetherness, accountability, determination, courage and self-esteem have to come back. People blessed with those attributes must be willing to serve as caring role models for those who lack them.

With that in mind, Sacramento Food Bank Services has grown over the past 20 years, from a place where the hungry can meet their need to be fed, to a refuge for people with the will to repair broken lives. We've seen that near miracles can happen when two worlds – the economically comfortable and the disadvantaged – break down the barriers between them and together tackle chronic social ills.

Our Mother-Baby program dispenses formula and diapers, but it also provides young parents with advice in nutrition, parenting and basic life skills lacked by so many.

A reading program for illiterate adults is helping many cross the chasm from a state of shame and chronic unemployment to self-esteem and job opportunities. Havens Transitional Housing, a program made possible by the donation and purchase of 12 homes, provides transitional living accommodations for the previously homeless. But along with a roof comes a mentor to train the resident in budgeting and household management, parenting and job skills. We provide free clothing and free classes – from tenant rights to budget cooking and smart shopping. The core of our volunteers is senior citizens, who find meaning in a program that doesn't belittle or entertain them, but values their dedication and skills.

We haven't begun to eradicate poverty in our city, but many good people are making a difference. With nearly 800 volunteers, Sacramento Food Bank Services is now going beyond just providing handouts to giving people the tools they need to better

their own lives. Our recycling program employs formerly homeless people and teaches job skills so people can lift themselves out of the cycle of poverty.

Today, Sacramento Food Bank Services continues to build a program of mentoring – where comfortable and successful residents share the good fortune of their education and self-discipline with people who have had only bad breaks. We are recycling waste, and in the process hiring people who need the chance to recycle their lives. And we are teaching families to learn together in a safe, loving environment.

Six years ago, I left my Oak Park parish to become pastor of a tiny brick church at the foot of a levee on the Sacramento river. When I left, it occurred to me that I'd probably not had a solid night's sleep in the prior 13 years — so pressing were the needs of the people in that neighborhood.

My new church, St. Joseph's in Clarksburg, is 14 miles and a 15-minute drive from the guns, sirens and long lines of the needy at our Food Bank. It feels as if it is 1,000 miles away.

I do some administrative work for Sacramento Food Bank Services in rural tranquility, by corn fields, grape vineyards and the river. At night I am blessed with silence interrupted only by crickets and the occasional barking of my dogs. But every day I return to Oak Park, where I am truly blessed with job fulfillment. Each morning as I drive to work I know the day will bring:

- 2,500 people for food
- 100 families for clothing
- 100 moms with their babies, needing formula, diapers and special care
- 45 students and their volunteer teachers to our literacy center
- 12 families being housed and mentored
- 10,000 pounds of food distributed from our warehouse
- 130 volunteers showing up for work.

Through the development of: 800 volunteers, 4,500 donors, warehouses, dwelling houses, trucks, forklifts, refrigerators and freezers, tremendous buying power and prayerful persuasion we are accomplishing what experts tell us is a $10 million a year operation. We do all this work with slightly over a million dollars in cash, 93 percent of which comes from local individuals and businesses. Less than seven percent of our funding comes from federal, state and local government. That is in stark contrast to many charities nationwide, which rely on government for much of their funding.

Our fundraising works because our appeals

come from the heart, not from boiler room operations. Among the ranks of our volunteers and staff are many Catholics, answering the call to volunteer through their parishes, but also Protestants and Jews and the religiously unaffiliated. All are personally dedicated to our purpose, and most feel they are called by God to volunteer.

We've developed a complex, multifaceted organization to tackle complex, multifaceted problems, and the potential to grow remains unlimited. But the secret to our success is simple. It boils down to people making the effort to uplift their community, and finding ways to better themselves in the process.

This book traces the evolution of our programs and of my philosophy of serving the poor. Over the years, as you'll see by looking at the dates of my letters, poverty's face has changed. No longer are the lines outside of our food locker comprised only of the addicted, the mentally ill or abused souls who have always scavenged for the scraps of America's bounty. Today, we see many from the once "solid" working class, whose security is a casualty of the much publicized downsizing of the U.S. job market. In California in the 1990s, the income gap between rich and poor has widened faster than anywhere else in the nation, not because the rich have gotten richer, but because the poor have grown more plentiful, and poorer.

Unfortunately, our programs have developed because needs have increased. Our goal at SFBS would be to empower the poor to the extent that we would be put out of business, but that dream is not likely to come true in my lifetime.

Meanwhile, I truly believe programs that we have at SFBS could be developed in any community where caring people are dedicated to tackling the problems of poverty. Perhaps if, like my mother, we all believed the poor were sent to us by Divine Providence, we might never turn our backs on the daunting task of helping others.

Fr. Dan Madigan

Fifty-two years combined volunteer service (l. to r.) Floyd Ahern, Don Rund, Ed DeWinter

FEEDING THE HUNGRY

THE FOOD LOCKER AND SUNDAY LUNCH

SEPTEMBER 1984

Dear Friends:

Even though more Americans went hungry last winter than at any time since the Great Depression, public outcry has been only minimal. This is so because few people fully realize what is taking place in regard to the poor.

Some believe that the poor are somehow themselves to blame for their poverty. Others claim that many of the poor are con artists who rip off food lockers and cheese giveaways while they own fancy cars. A segment may very well be guilty of this. But the vast majority who call on us for food are truly hurting and it is of them I wish to speak.

A very large number of those who come to our food locker/soup kitchen are, in my opinion, chronically disturbed. Their mental illness is immediately evident. Character and personality disorders render them unable to cope with the demands of daily life. Some can be heard muttering to themselves or answering voices that only they can hear. Others would willingly share their delusions and hallucinations if they could find listeners. All seem to be crying out for appropriate psychiatric help.

Another definable group at the food locker gate are the alcoholics. Usually they are unattached, middle-aged men. Alcohol is their central frame of reference, impermanence is their way of life. They get kicked out of hotels, frequent the missions and Salvation Army, sleep out in weeds and occasionally spend a night in jail. As a rule they stay in their own areas, for they are well aware of the stigma they carry as "bums." Most are burdened with a deep sense of personal failure and have abandoned any reasonable hope of re-creating themselves. Alcohol is their only friend, providing them with some measure of euphoria and optimism, dulling the loneliness, unhappiness and sense of social inadequacy. That eventually takes its toll and can be easily seen from their tattered clothing, their absence of self-esteem and their chronic health problems.

I find it difficult to believe that human beings who are reduced to foraging in dumpsters, collecting aluminum cans and selling their blood for existence are taking advantage of food lockers.

Next come the neighborhood parents who are often accompanied by their ragged, unkempt children. Born poor, they have yet to escape the clutch of poverty. Their most determined efforts to raise themselves are defeated by the miserable conditions in which they are obliged to live. Their rents are excessive, their neighborhoods degrading, their public amenities inferior, their surroundings discourage any initiative.

I believe no sane person would line up and wait outside a food locker window for a few loaves of bread or a can of beans if he had money in his pocket or the wherewithal to live comfortably.

I see very little excuse, therefore, to refuse anyone and I feel we have never been "ripped off." If people give false information in trying to obtain food for themselves and their families, can we say they are not justified?

Day after day, the poor keep coming to our food locker. I have watched them for nine years now, and the only difference I see of late is the huge increase in numbers. The line is always made up of the same type of people: the mentally ill, the alcoholics, the chronically unemployed, the unskilled workers, the deserted wives, the physically and socially handicapped, the street people, the badly housed, the ex-prisoners, the educationally deprived.

What are we to do? St. Paul stood by uninvolved as people stoned the martyr Stephen. He spent his life regretting it. We are all responsible when people suffer from hunger, cold, oppression and hatred. We cannot be apathetic. We cannot stand idly by. We are not powerless. We CAN make a difference!

With every good wish to you,

Fr. Dan Madigan

January 1985

Dear Friends:

Occasionally I stand outside the dispensing window and talk with the people who wait in line there for food. I find it impossible to categorize them or even their attitudes. They come from all walks of life – men and women of all ages, races and cultures. Now and then I see a few who are happy, life-loving, even boisterous. But on the whole, their faces are tense with anxiety or saddened by one or another of the many kinds of pain.

Here are desperate, disappointed people with no ties, few roots and frequently no shelter. Loneliness is prevalent among them and some have even chosen to walk alone – like those who bring their whole world stuffed into a shopping cart that has become their mobile home. These are people of loss – loss of social connections, of health, of self-esteem. All they know is menial work, for they are also people of lacks – lack of education, lack of skills.

While I stand in line with these people, I am keenly aware of a segment among them that has seen social workers and programs come and go without giving them any deep down help or understanding. This has apparently made them quite callous.

I make it a point to stand on the other side of the window too, sometimes, looking over the shoulder of the volunteer who must receive requests and evaluate needs. I am sure that the person who sits at the window has the most difficult of all volunteer tasks. For how is one to cope with the litany of disappointment and anxiety, and stay highly motivated? How can one remain zealous and not burn out under the stress?

I guess hard work done with conviction and enthusiasm will never cause stress or burn-out. I am sure we create stress for ourselves. And I think we cause stress for ourselves at the window when we begin to feel we must try to change significantly the people we meet there. There is no possible way we can change them. We can only change our own evaluation of them. If we try to imagine that they are drowning in a lake and that we are rescuers who throw a rope, pull them out and put them on solid ground for at least a little while, then perhaps we will feel our job is meaningful and that we are accomplishing a great deal.

However, if we ask ourselves why these people are drowning, why they are in the lake, why they are outside the window, why they lie, giving false names and information to get more food than they are entitled to, such questions can cause us tremendous frustration. We can easily understand why they lie to get more food. But once a volunteer goes heavily into the "why" of their need to beg in this great country of ours, or the "why" of their inadequacies, then that volunteer should probably move to another aspect of the Food Locker service. The window will become far too stressful.

Many times I've asked myself if it would be more Christian to fight for people's rights than give someone a basket of food. Is it more Christian to attack the sources of suffering than to relieve the suffering itself? These are big questions that are nice to ponder while sitting on a commission of social concern. But I think these questions are above and beyond reality for us. The real question is what are we doing about the poor here and now? How are we touching their lives? Of course, there should not be any hungry people in this country. The point is, there are. They are here. They are in Oak Park. They are outside the window, looking in.

God bless you and take care of yourself,

Fr. Dan Madigan

Dear Friends:

There is an old Irish saying: "Go often to the house of your friend, for weeds choke the un-used path." In aligning yourself with our work you became not only our friend but a member of the Food Bank family. That's why you are getting this letter. As a member of our family you are entitled to hear all the family problems.

The numbers we feed daily have multiplied enormously since we added the government com-modities this past January. This means we reach more of the city's poor, but it also adds greatly to the demand for our usual balanced meals, which these government provisions only supplement. With over two hundred people a day in the Oak Park food locker line, we are very hard pressed. And we still have Del Paso Heights, Meadowview and Rancho Cordova food lockers to supply, plus two soup kitchens. Canned goods are dwindling, as are staples. We have desperate need for baby food and formula. Can you help us even more than you are presently doing?

God bless you always. As the Spanish say, "Dios lo paga," which means, loosely, "God will re-pay."

With every good wish,

Fr. Dan Madigan

Dear Friends:

Reverend Mother Bridget O'Shaughnessy had a policy for her Sacramento-based convent that all beggars coming to their door would receive a dollar. She felt that any one of these hurting people might very well be St. Peter in disguise. Her wisdom was questioned one day by a young novice who claimed that the man at the door was very drunk, could not possibly be St. Peter and was not deserving of help. Reverend Mother's response was "Sister, give the man the dollar – he may very well be St. Patrick."

At our food outlets we see them all – St. Patricks and St. Peters. Some have caused their own misfortunes. The majority have not.

Sacramento Food Bank Services distributes over $200,000 worth of food a month. It takes long hours of work to convert tractor-trailer loads of loose commodities (e.g. beans, rice, flour, powdered milk, fruits and vegetables) into small packages and then place them in the hands of hungry families. Yet, thank God, this is a daily occurrence. The people who do this need your prayers.

With every good wish,

Fr. Dan Madigan

My Dear Friends:

Many years of inner city living have shown me lots of misery – poverty, hunger and depriva-
tion, filth, disease and mental illness, illiteracy, unemployment and latchkey kids.

Dysfunctional people, incapacitated families and the de-institutionalized mentally ill have
been with us from the beginning. They still are. But now they have new companions.

Today's food line is mostly made up of hard-working, low-paid family people, fixed income
elderly and the neatly dressed and highly embarrassed unemployed. All have the same to say
– that no matter how they stretch their income it will not cover rent, utilities, medical care,
clothing and food for their entire family.

Our police chief is amazed at what's happening. His statistics show that when the first six
months of 1991 are compared to those for 1990 there is an increase in armed robbery of 32
percent. I also am flabbergasted to see that when we look at the same period of time in our
Sacramento Food Bank operation, we see a 50 percent increase in the number of needy
people we are serving.

Gone are the days for mere social questioning and lukewarm community concern. Immediate
action is needed. The galling chains of poverty and illiteracy that so often shackle people to
crime and even push them into gangs and narcotics need to be broken. These people need
mentors. If your family life is working, please consider helping us and becoming a mentor to a
hurting family. Mentors show that an alternative lifestyle is within reach. Mentors work with
families on their journey of change. Mentors help them develop the emotional and intellec-
tual powers to make this journey.

Because the need is so urgent, I know you will help if you can.

May our good God truly bless you,

Fr. Dan Madigan

Dear Friends:

I have fond memories of 1993. Eight hundred of you gave us countless hours of volunteer work. Four thousand of you contributed a million dollars in cash. And our agency delivered $10 million of social services.

Yes, it's a real privilege to captain a ship where dollar bills are turned into tens. And where we don't just believe in miracles but watch them happen before our eyes.

Our multiplication formula worked well on the day prior to Thanksgiving. We fed 2,000 families. We gave each a $50 box of food. And we did the entire job for $5,300.

Multiplication worked better at Christmas. Two thousand kids received gifts from us, and all at zero cost to our operation. And, yes, the miracle is still going on. Generous Sacramento businesses, offices, schools, churches, clubs and organizations are presently filling barrels with food for our Holiday Spirit of Giving Drive. We expect to net 300,000 pounds of food which, if purchased at market value, would cost close to $300,000.

Today I officiated at a funeral. I read Psalm 23. I listened to the prophet say, "Though I walk in the valley of darkness I fear no evil for You are with me." As I drove back to the Food Bank I found myself thinking how true that prayer is. And why should I, who have the Lord rooting for me and you, my friends, who are actively playing on our team, worry about 1994?

May God bless you all,

Fr. Dan Madigan

MY SEMINARY TRAINING GAVE ME ANSWERS to

all questions. And while thirty years in the priesthood have

removed that secure platform, these same thirty years have introduced

me to a much kinder God than the one I knew as a youngster. Since childhood I

have regarded religion and spirituality as synonymous. And while this thinking may

very well be true, years of working at Sacramento Food Bank Services have exposed me to

numerous people who are deeply spiritual but who are not associated with any given reli-

gious group.

One of my spiritual mentors is Fr. Joseph Girzone, author of <u>Joshua</u>. Here is what he has

to say about religion: "For sixteen centuries we have associated religion with church build-

ings and institutional structures. When we think of the Church, we instinctively think of bricks and steel, of dignitaries in flowing robes and ornate ritual. Since childhood these images have been engraved in our memories. They are changeless, immutable, everlasting. To think of altering them shakes people's faith.

"Yet, in all the Gospel stories Jesus' way of life and the flow of His teachings had nothing to do with buildings or structures or complex rituals. He did attend the synagogue faithfully. He did attend the temple services for the sacred feasts. But He once remarked that true worship is not in buildings but in the sincerity of our lives and the devotion of our hearts.

"His followers for over two hundred years followed that simple way of worshiping God by gathering in unadorned family liturgies and caring for each other's needs. But then came the Roman Emperors who decided to do God a favor and gather Christ's followers into what became the imperial religion of Rome. From then on Christianity became a thing of grandeur and pageantry. The simple Jesus was lost, His message became enshrined in finely chiseled theological concepts.

"On rare occasions through the centuries, the Spirit of God managed to break through the hard crust of religion and inspire individuals, usually simple, docile souls, to discover for themselves the real Jesus and to act out in their own lives the lifestyle set forth by the Master. St. Francis was one, Damian the Leper another, as well as Mother Teresa and Gandhi."

I thank God for the blessing of SFBS. Without the daily exposure to the needy I might have become isolated in my religion, preaching Christ's message rather than trying on a daily basis to carry it out. I might have felt my priest's collar, my performance of ritual duties, to be sufficient evidence of my faith. Instead I was challenged, my certitude rocked, my notion of God and God's love expanded. Along the way, He blessed me with friends devoted to carrying out SFBS' mission, with contributors when money was short, with volunteers and dedicated staff.

Most priests aren't trained for inner city work, and I was no exception. It is possible to naively enter a world such as Oak Park and miss the whole picture for a long time. I learned the language of the streets by osmosis. The needs of the community were apparent to anyone with half a desire to observe them. Food was the most obvious, most basic need. After Mass on Sundays, and at all hours of the day and night, indigent people rang our rectory doorbell asking for bread, a meal, or money to buy their children a hamburger.

Starting a small food locker and soup kitchen required no great stretch of my organizational ability, but resources were tight. Members of our Oak Park parish jumped to the task, and within a couple of years we were bursting at the seams. At that point, we had refrigerators everywhere: on the grounds, in the church school, under the auditorium stage, on top of the stage, in the corridors, in mobile trailers. Every inch we had was devoted to food storage.

I credit my dear friend Charles (Chuck) Sylva for having the vision that got us from that state of affairs to where we are today. Chuck was a successful commercial real estate broker, a very unassuming, very devout man with powerful connections in the community but absolutely no hint of bravado about him. When we were cramped and serving food out of a little trailer, I asked him his ideas on how we could expand. He said he would think about it while I was back in Ireland for a visit.

While I was still away, I got a phone call from the principal of our school, John Healey.

"You're going to come back and find someone seated in your chair," he told me. That didn't go over too well. I was wondering how anyone would get a key to my office, and I muttered something along the lines of, "that's a bit much." Healey laughed and indicated I was in for a great surprise.

When I landed back in Sacramento, Chuck picked me up at the airport. He drove into town, and before dropping me off at Immaculate Conception, took me a block away to the abandoned, 30,000-square-foot Arata warehouse. This building, once Sacramento's first major supermarket and the first push-cart market in the West, was a rat-infested and boarded-up testament to the neighborhood's decline.

"That's what we need," Chuck said, pointing to the massive structure.

"Oh, no, that's far too big!" I responded. It took up nearly half the block.

Then my dear friend gave me an even bigger shock. "I've decided to take a year off, and work with you," he said. "We'll get this building, and move the food lockers over here."

At age 39, when he was one of Sacramento's top real estate brokers, Chuck Sylva took leave of his lucrative career for the entire year of 1987.

"There's more to life than making money for your own benefit," he told *The Sacramento Bee* when the story hit the business pages.

Chuck's goal was to raise the money to buy the warehouse and really help SFBS begin to take off as a social service center. He knew I had great intentions, but lacked the business sophistication to get the funding we'd need.

Within a few days we had our Bishop, Francis Quinn, out there. He looked at the building and gave me a loan of $400,000. I made a commitment we would pay it off. We got a loan for another $350,000 from the bank, and bought the building.

We could only afford to do a little bit with the building at a time, and it took most of a year to finance and refurbish it. John Healey and I spent all our spare moments along with parishioners, remodeling the Arata Center bit by bit. I couldn't even imagine a time would come when we would use all of that space, and need even more.

Meanwhile, Chuck said it was time for us to be hitting the streets to raise the cash to

pay for this building. One morning he told me he was taking me to visit a friend of his, Chris Steele, who was then partner of a successful development company.

Until that point, everything was going fine. I was secure within my own Catholic community, doing the work with the poor I felt called to do. I had lots of help from my parishioners past and present, and Chuck's great gift of time and business experience. However, I had no connections in the community at large, certainly not in the business community, and no idea of how to develop them. Despite my ability to get up and tell stories and give sermons, I'm terribly shy in such foreign circumstances. I'd never asked

anyone for money in my life. I had no stomach for it. I suppose I'd had to make general appeals in church for donations, but I couldn't ask a friend for even $5. I just couldn't do it.

So we were driving down the freeway on this maiden voyage, when Chuck said, "You'll meet my friend, and I want you to ask him for money."

"Oh, gosh, no," I said. "He's *your* friend. *You* ask him."

"Oh, no-no-no," Chuck responded. "I'm just doing the introducing. This is your project, and you're going to have to start doing the asking."

I can remember at that point feeling very very uneasy, very, very uptight. I was thinking, "I can't do this. There's no way. It'll kill me."

Finally I said to Chuck, "How much shall I ask him for?"

He said, "I want you to ask him for $100,000."

Honestly, I could have asked him to pull off to the side of the freeway so I could throw up!

When we arrived at Chris Steele's office he was very friendly. He told us how he got his start from humble beginnings, and asked about our project and the purchase of the Arata building. He and Chuck were talking real estate this and development that, and all of a sudden he turned to me and said, "Father, what can I do for you? I know you've come to me for help."

So, I looked at the man and I don't know

how, but I blurted out, "Could you give us $100,000?" He looked back at me and without blinking an eye said, "Well, I think we can, but I need to talk to my partner about it." So we left, and that was it.

It was only a matter of weeks when a $50,000 check arrived in the mail. I couldn't believe it. I just couldn't believe it. The check came along with a note: "You'll get the other $50,000 when the cows come home." Well, the cows came home rather quickly, and within a couple of months we were well on our way towards paying back our loan. Because of that, Chris Steele will always be my financial hero. While people have come along and done enormous things for SFBS since, two people, Chris Steele and David Allen, did something for me when SFBS was penniless and owned nothing. Steele, who gave me that first check, and Allen, who soon afterwards donated the proceeds of the sale of a house, showed they believed in our vision.

From then on it was easier to go out and ask, and we started getting checks and more checks. We passed the collection plate at churches, and had teams of eight to ten people asking for donations from people as they left church. A crusty old fund-raiser we hired to advise us was familiar with raising money for the Catholic Church. When it came time to make our appeal to St. Mel's parish in the suburban community of Fair Oaks, he convinced us to try a different tactic.

Father Richard Doheny agreed to let us set up tables with volunteers, serve coffee and cookies down in the church school after mass. At services, when it came time for me to talk about our project, I didn't directly ask for a collection. Instead, I urged the congregation to read our pamphlets, and said there would be volunteers down at the school happy to tell them more. Now, I knew this was a wealthy congregation, and expected I could walk out of there with perhaps $4,000 in pledges. But dozens of people accepted our invitation for coffee and a chat with our volunteers, and I walked out of that church at the end of the day with $80,000 in pledges! That experience taught me a valuable lesson. Sitting down and talking face-to-face with a person, personally sharing your excitement about a program, is a far more effective fundraising strategy than simply passing a basket after a speech.

Chuck, in addition to being a brilliant planner and businessman, helped me build my own foundation for fundraising and developing strong community ties. First, he recommended I join the Rotary Club of Sacramento. Now, there are over 27,000 Rotary Clubs in the world, and Rotary of Sacramento is number 15 in size. It has nearly 500 active members. Walking into a meeting was, for me, a very frightening experience. I felt, "I'm different. I'm not wearing a business suit and tie, I'm not in real estate or banking, I'm a priest, and there's no way I'll ever fit in." Even though the club's members were very friendly, and seemed a wonderfully generous bunch of community-minded people, I had such difficulty overcoming my own shyness I resigned after just a couple of months of meetings.

I wrote a letter saying I had to resign on account of my duties and such, but I confess it was a lie. It was because I just didn't feel comfortable. The club was so generous, though, it wrote back, and instead of accepting my resignation, gave me a leave of absence. I was overwhelmed with how nice they were. I thought, "If they're that kind, then I'm going to try and get courage enough to go back." Later, I even got the courage to tell the true story to the club's president, Dave Murphy.

So, with the help of Chuck Sylva, John Healey and the generous people at Rotary, I broke out of my cloistered world and into the community at large. My newsletters about the work we were doing at the Food Bank were sent to hundreds of people, then thousands. Hundreds more personal thank-you notes were required as the newsletters generated donations.

As we built our funding base and got the community more involved in our work, we also firmed up our philosophy.

Above all, we wanted to serve the poor, but not to participate in the pauperization of the poor. In other words, we believe we should treat each person with the dignity each person deserves. So often, volunteer agencies in service to the poor take a "loose" approach to their management. If they say they'll be open from 10-12, they might be open from 10:15 to 11:45. After all, they reason, the staff are volunteers. Goods are donated and donations may run out.

I find such an approach absolutely unacceptable. It requires the poor, so often forced to wait in long lines, to wait even more, or be turned away without notice. The core of my management style at SFBS has always been: "Do exactly what we say we'll do, at the time we say we'll do it." Anything else sends a message to the poor that they deserve less.

I'm a stickler on this issue, and sometimes lose my cool when I see people taking a more lax approach to their responsibilities. We have to ask ourselves, I think, what message we send by our behavior. Is handing out food simply a way for us to feel benevolent? Are we content to hand out food as long as the poor keep "their place"? Or are we really responsible for giving more than just handouts?

As our food programs grew, these questions loomed in my mind. And I was reminded over and over again that Fr. Girzone was right when he suggested that religion is not the only arena for God's work.

A DAY AT THE
FOOD LOCKERS

AT 6 A.M., JAN GIVAS UNLOCKS AN IRON gate, looks around warily and pulls her aging maroon Volvo into the dark rear parking lot of the Food Bank warehouse. Another key opens a heavy steel door into the building, where she flips on a light and says hello to Socks, the Food Bank mascot. A black cat with, predictably, white feet, Socks wears an official, laminated collar tag identifying him as an SFBS worker. Socks has been on the job all night, prowling for any mice that might scamper between pallets of rice and beans, donated Milk Duds and pickles, ramen noodles and vegetables.

A tall woman with black hair pulled back into a ponytail, Jan pulls a blue work smock over her comfortable, red knit pants outfit, and signs the daily visitor's roster. As the food locker program director, she's not paid to come into work until 7 a.m. But Jan is an accomplished player in the business of feeding the poor, and operates by one of its key

rules: getting there early means a crack at the best food, and a shorter time waiting for it to be loaded onto your truck.

"There," in this instance, is another, larger warehouse complex – the Senior Gleaners, Inc. food distribution center 15 minutes north of the SFBS warehouse in the suburb of North Highlands. The operation, run by senior citizen volunteers, is the Sacramento Food Bank's main supplier of salvaged and surplus food.

Givas trades her Volvo keys for the keys of a donated 1984 Chevy truck – one of 19 vehicles in the SFBS fleet – locks the parking lot gate and drives up Interstate 80 to arrive at Senior Gleaners by 6:30 a.m. Already, the tiny front office of the Gleaners' main warehouse office is bustling. A half-dozen people from smaller charities are waiting, order slips in hand, for their number to be called when food loading begins at 7:00.

"Some get here as early as 4 a.m., and sit there until 7:00," Givas says. "Many times I'm here by 4:30, so I can get done and get back to the Food Bank."

On this September day, Givas picks up a duplicate order slip at the front desk of the main warehouse office, and takes it down a narrow hallway to start dealing.

"What you got, Isles?" she asks Isles Lawson, a longtime Gleaners volunteer who processes food orders. Givas trusts Lawson to tell her what produce is good, what baked goods are in, and what's available for free as opposed to deeply discounted. The Gleaners purchase some discounted food and allocate it to charities according to their size. Charities are asked to give donations to help defray the cost of purchased items.

"Anything for sale, we get for six cents a pound," explains Givas. "Things that are allocated to us, we have to take, for example, a pallet of cereal for $40. That's 2,500 pounds of cereal – a lot, but it goes fast."

"Any cauliflower?" Givas asks. Lawson checks a computerized list and nods yes. "Onions?" Lawson tells her they are particularly crummy that day, so Givas leaves them off the list.

Morning pickup at the Gleaners' is a job that each day yields different results. Givas' final list reads: cucumbers, miscellaneous pastry, pretzels, Lucky Stores salvage (canned goods and perishable foods near their expiration date), tomato products, orange soda, dry baby food, frozen mashed potatoes, potato wedges, Ocean Spray juice. Givas tells Lawson she's interested only in free food, and shows her the list to double check that nothing on it will be billed.

"I want to beat my last year's budget," she explains. "That was $280,000, but $90,000-some of it was FEMA (food provided by the Federal Emergency Management Administration), where you have to buy macaroni and cheese, beans and rice, ramen. Last year we did real well on that." That $280,000 was stretched to provide 8.5 million meals – $10 worth of food for each dollar spent.

Givas, referred to by her co-workers as the "Sgt. Bilko" of the food locker, barters, ca-joles, and deals to get more for less. Her budget covers four food lockers – SFBS' main food locker and warehouse in Oak Park, the Del Paso Heights Food Locker, and two affiliates. The affiliates, one run out of a Catholic church serving the Hispanic community in South Central Sacramento and one run by a Methodist Church in North Sacramento, have their own volunteers but are given food and computer support by SFBS staff. SFBS' two "company stores," in Oak Park and Del Paso Heights, are open five days a week from 10 a.m. until 2 p.m., with the help of 250 volunteers.

"Not too long ago a gentleman called me from the 49er truck stop, telling me a trucker had a pallet of canned goods he couldn't deliver somewhere else, because the store couldn't use them and the guy didn't want to drive the pallet back to L.A. A pallet is 197 cases, with 12 cans to a case.

"I said I'd be glad to take it, and by the way, if he sees anyone else in that kind of predicament, send him my way! Now I'm getting calls continually. We got a whole pallet of green beans, peas, carrots and corn, and a pallet of fresh salmon on ice from Pacific Fresh Seafood Company. They couldn't ship it back to Washington, the truck stop guy called us, and we had a two-hour window to pick it up. We were giving out fresh salmon that day!

"I also barter," Givas says, a gleam in her eye as she reveals some of her better deals. When gourmet coffee beans are donated, she gives them to a local soup kitchen that

serves hot coffee each morning to long lines of homeless men. In return for 40 pounds of coffee, she gets a bin – 2,500 pounds – of small canned goods. "Sometimes I can get two bins," she says with a satisfied smile.

"I always come out ahead, because I've got things others can't get, like small diapers. We get more of those than any other size. I'll have pallets and pallets of small diapers, so I'll trade them. Anything I can get for other food lockers, I can share. We take from Gleaners anything we can get. Then people call me and ask if I have anything we can't use, like bleach or Comet. I got two full pallets of unlabeled, stewed tomatoes for half a pallet of Dawn dish soap. Good trade?" She winks.

By the time Givas gets outside the Glean-

ers' office, the sun is up and an elderly man in dungarees and goosedown vest is heading toward her truck with a forklift carrying 250 pounds of cucumbers. Already loaded are 720 loaves of bread, 20 boxes of pastry and 20 boxes of cauliflower, each 26 pounds.

This shipment is headed for the Del Paso Heights Food Locker – a triple-wide trailer that sits on the parking lot of a boarded up, graffiti-covered Asian grocery. The unprepossessing operation is one of the busiest food lockers in California, serving up to 18,000 people a month, over half of whom are children.

When Givas arrives in the Del Paso Heights parking lot with her loaded truck at 8 a.m., assistant manager Art Thompson is waiting. At 71, the wiry retired warehouseman from Modesto volunteers at least 40 hours a week, unloading the pallets of food with a forklift, stocking and restocking the shelves.

"It keeps me from sitting around the house," Thompson explains. "The food locker is close to my residence, and the job is about what I did in my old work, so everything just kind of fell in line."

By 8:30 a.m. a half-dozen more senior volunteers arrive. On this day the workers are veteran volunteers from McClellan Air Force Base, retirees and widows who have been coming once a week for ten years.

"If you add up the ages of all of us working here, you'd have a lotta years," says volunteer Helen Brandenburg, "six times 70, for starters." A round-faced, cheerful woman, she moves quickly along a table piled with canned goods and produce, filling a bag with each item.

One of the volunteers suggests starting the day with a prayer. They gather in a circle and thank God for the health and willingness of the volunteers, for the friendships that have grown through their service, for the donated food. And they ask for patience and stamina in the day ahead.

In the same room where volunteers are gathered in a circle, shelves are stocked with bags already loaded with basic, non-perishable items – ramen noodles, rice and beans – arranged by family size with three-day servings for one to six persons. Volunteers like Brandenburg add to these bags the daily allotment of perishable and salvaged items brought that day from Senior Gleaners.

In an adjacent room, Givas and another volunteer sit in front of computers, where all visitors to the Food Bank are kept on file.

A list of phonetically spelled common Russian expressions: "How are you? Have a Nice Day, Thank You, You're Welcome," is posted by the window – a sign of Sacramento's burgeoning population of refugees from former Eastern Bloc countries.

"How are you doing this morning?" Givas asks the first in a line of some 45 people waiting when the window opens at 10 a.m. "Fine. You?" mumbles a lean, stringy-haired woman. She hands Givas her driver's license and a slip with her name, address, the number of people in her family and identifying her as a recipient of Aid to Families with Dependent Children. Givas calls the name up on the computer screen, checking to see that the woman hasn't yet come for a bag of food that month.

Because food stocks are limited, families are restricted to a three-day supply of food, plus government commodities such as butter and rice, once a month. Addresses are checked to ensure customers are using the food closet in their zip code, and computers at SFBS' outlets cross-check so that people aren't getting commodities from more than one food closet. Clients who come more than once in a month are given bread only, and an apology for the limit.

The slips received and checked at the computer are delivered to volunteers who fill brown grocery bags according to family size, then pass them to recipients at a second window.

Two volunteers work at the computers, one or two fill the bags, one hands out the bags, and one takes produce from crates and boxes and repackages it into smaller portions to be put into the grocery bags. Once the windows are open, the hectic process begins. For four hours, there is no let-up.

A volunteer relieves Givas at the computer, so Givas helps another volunteer empty cases of frozen broccoli and carrots into small plastic bags. The bags, donated by a company that uses them for computer chip boards, are crinkly, "electrostatic" material, and must be secured with rubber bands. It takes about 20 minutes to repackage a box of the frozen vegetables. Eight more boxes to go. Givas scoops the vegetables with an empty can and wraps them with the deft movements of an assembly line worker.

The tedium of the task is broken with pleasant chatter. A friendly dispute arises: are Sacramentans more generous than other Californians? Brandenberg thinks so, another volunteer disagrees.

Art Thompson moves another load of boxes to the table, stacking the empties along a wall.

"You gotta watch some people like flies on a meatskin," he mutters, referring to a recipient who'd tried to get a double allotment of free butter. Does he get frustrated at such incidents, enough to think it's not worth coming in at 8 a.m. everyday? "Nah,"

Thompson says, back to stocking the shelves. "There's too much work to do."

Across town at the Oak Park Food Locker, SFBS' "flagship store," the daily doling out of food to the needy is a noisier version of the operation at the Del Paso Heights food locker. The bag donated to families that day contained an eclectic but healthy mix – a "good haul," by veteran volunteers' standards. Sacks on the shelves, marked by family size, contain lentils, canned tuna, canned vegetables, ramen dried noodle soup, boxed macaroni and cheese. Volunteers add to each bag cucumbers, jelly, mayonnaise, mixed fresh vegetables, a bottle of red wine marinade sauce, oatmeal, margarine, peach-kiwi flavored juice, bread and cake or cookies. Each item is stacked on a long table. A case of fresh purple grapes, sweet and juicy, but perhaps too small for market sale, must be packed, handful by sticky handful, into plastic bags.

Volunteers walk the length of the table, filling bags. Federal commodities – beans, rice, macaroni and butter – are added at the end of long table for those whose computer slips say they are eligible. The bags are filled to bulging by the time they are brought to a second window and handed to recipients.

At the computer window, a retired advertising executive works a volunteer stint checking IDs and explaining the system. His voice mingles with volunteers' chatter inside the warehouse, shouts and children's shrieks from the line outside. Empty cardboard boxes are tossed in a pile, grocery bags

crinkle and recipients' names are shouted when their food has been bagged.

"Have you been here before, ma'am?" asks the volunteer. "Oh, okay, let me put you in the computer today. Okay, that's Tiffany? 25th Street? Do you have any children living with you?" Squeals from children in line drown out the answer. (Next!)

"Okay, guys, every time you come, please bring ID," the volunteer continues. "Something that shows your name, address and Social Security number. Okay. Felicia? That's two adults, ma'am? And that's one, two, three, four, five children? Okay. They'll call your name, ma'am. You're welcome." (Next!) "Hi. How are you? Anita? And how about your children, ma'am? Okay. I can give you food today, but what you have to do next time is bring ID for everyone you're asking food for in the whole family." (Next!) "May I see your ID, sir? (I don't have it.) We had that same problem last time, it says here, sir. Help us out, okay? Bring us a letter, or something. Canceled mail, parking tickets, even arrest warrants. I'm easy." (Next!) "Quantos Ninos? Uno? Social Security numero, solamente."

It's a litany to which SFBS director Jay Schenirer subjects himself, at least a few times each week, to keep him in touch with the sheer numbers and need. "The reality is, there's not that much difference between me and the people in line," Schenirer says. "The best thing I ever did was be born to my parents."

The food that fills the bags handed out by volunteers comes from the brand of wheeling and dealing for charity Givas enjoys, and through constant networking with manufacturers and the local business community.

Food that manufacturers can't distribute across the country a month before its expiration date often is donated, and shows up in food locker bags well before it has expired. "To you and me, the expiration date is a month away, but to them, it's not saleable," Schenirer explains.

The same goes for cereal or soft drinks promoting the Super Bowl once the game is over, house brands that have gone out of business, or products whose labels are misspelled. "To manufacturers, it's an hour of production lost because of a typo. To us, it's baby formula for months."

If a manufacturer, grocery store or caterer calls with a donation, one of SFBS' 17 donated trucks or vans is dispatched to pick it up. When local grocers and businesses hold their annual SFBS Spirit of Giving holiday food drive, placing barrels for donated food in building lobbies, banks and stores, the Food Bank nets some 300,000 pounds of non-perishable foods.

SFBS buys "substandard" food, that wouldn't be sold on the open market. Bean "splits" that are good, but look ugly, are purchased along with rice kernels, called "second heads" that cook up mushier than whole kernel rice but are just as nutritious. The advantage to those products is the price – from 11 to 15 cents a pound.

At the end of the month, when lines swell with people whose welfare or paychecks have been spent, the contents of the food locker's grocery bags may dwindle to rice, beans and slim pickings.

"About 60 percent of the people we deal with are under 12 years of age," the retired ad executive said. "It's hard. God, it gets real hard. The food we give out, it's not lobster tails and filet mignon, although the public would like to think that. The truth is, it's often crummy food. Days-old bread and imperfect produce. You wouldn't buy it."

The frustration of handing out too little to too many in need would be overwhelming for SFBS staff and volunteers, if it were not for the services that separate SFBS from most other food banks in the nation.

"The food line is an entree into our other programs," Fr. Dan explains. "We can't judge ourselves successful by just giving out more food. We have to help people get their lives together. Help them learn how to be parents, stay healthy, get sober, feel good about themselves. If we see a young mother in the food line, we refer her to the Mother-Baby program. If someone has trouble filling out their slip because they are illiterate, we can encourage them to go to our Reading Center. We have 100 mentors, and every day we're working on ways we can help people turn their lives around. The idea is to reach people from the food line, so they'll never have to come back."

SIX IN THE FOOD LINE

AT OAK PARK, THE LINE SNAKES THROUGH A crowded hallway, out to the sidewalk and around the Food Bank's warehouse. The hall-way, brightened by a mural of trees and flowers, is a cacophony of loud chatter, cry-ing children, shouts of outrage over various injustices, perceived or real. The Food Bank is at the center of a remarkably ethnically diverse neighborhood – 29 percent African-American, 26 percent Hispanic, 23 percent Caucasian and 20 percent Asian – and its clientele reflects the population.

A middle-aged African-American man clowns loudly and punches the air. He's a once-famous boxer, "Prince Albert," explains a Hispanic man, a recovering cocaine ad-dict, himself several feet behind the boxer in line.

An elderly Caucasian man hugs close to the wall, ignoring the crowd. By 10 a.m., when the flowered curtains are pulled back from the Food Bank window and fastened open with rubber bands, 45 people are wait-ing. Some appear embarrassed, others resigned, angry or impatient. Whatever se-ries of misfortunes and mistakes got them here, they seem to want to get away as quickly as possible. By afternoon on this day near the end of the month, the wait for a bag of free food will be 30 minutes.

Leona P., a 31-year-old mother, buckles the shoe of her 3-year-old son, then tucks her blouse neatly into her walking shorts. She's

been waiting 20 minutes for her turn at the window.

"It's been three or four months since I've been here," she explains quickly. What brings her here now? "This month, I had school clothes to buy, and then it was my oldest son's birthday, so getting him a present and everything put us behind."

She says she graduated from high school, attended college a couple of semesters, then worked delivering parts and as a cashier at an auto repair shop, "until I got pregnant and had to quit." Now she stays home and receives AFDC. She is unable to find afford-able day care for her 3-year-old, and wants to be home when her 9-year-old gets home from school. "He's hyper, and I sort of have to be on call," she explains.

Reyes L., 39, says he's a registered nurse who lost his job when he became addicted to cocaine. "I'm not working at this time, because I ran into a drug problem," he says. "I'm ready to go back to work now, but it's hard finding anything."

He complains that he's seen Food Bank vol-unteers question the identification of some in the line, offering only bread to those who return more than once a month.

"People have to realize, we don't want to be here," he says. "You wake up, look at the refrigerator and say, 'Damn, I got to go to the locker again.' "

His dream as a child was to play baseball for the St. Louis Cardinals. "But I grew up with an attitude," he says. "I was a tough little kid in the neighborhood. We felt it was our way or no way, and I got 8-balled by my coaches because of that. No way could I move ahead like that. After that, I became a 17-year-old parent." He says he lived with a girlfriend for nine years, went to college, then moved to Phoenix for a couple of years before returning to Sacramento to work and becoming addicted to rock cocaine.

"Now, I'm not on cocaine, but I'm not working," he says. "I'm homeless, living with a friend, with five kids and three adults in one house."It's time to get back into the system."

Robert B., 42, is a massive man with tattoos showing below the sleeves of his white T-shirt. "This is about my third visit," he says, waiting in line at the Del Paso Heights Food Locker. "But it's my first visit in about two years. "I was low on food. I have two kids, 13 and 14, I have to feed, plus my fiancée. I'm on SSI and it don't even stretch to the end of the month."

His 14-year-old son hangs back in line and looks away, embarrassed. "My rent is $480," the father continues, "and I only get $614. I'm unemployed and looking for work as an auto detailer or a cook. I've been out of work three years, first because I was incarcerated, then I've been in a drug rehab center. I've been out about two years and mostly self employed – I'll get maybe two days work or none at all. What's left over is nothing for food. You have your personal hygiene items to buy, you got your electric bills, that's $60-$70 a month, and $40-50 a month on gas. The phone is anywhere from zero to $100. Forget the clothes, and really forget the food. You don't have it, you're gonna get tired, so you come here. But I only come to the food closet when I need it."

Louise M., 31, is a high school drop-out who survives on General Assistance payments. "My kids are with their father, because I just came off of drug and alcohol rehab," she says, matter-of-factly. "I've been off 15 days. I'm looking for work, but there's not much to put on a resumé when you've been on drugs for years. I've done minor construction assistance and housekeeping. I started a training program, but missed my appointment, so here I am."

Jim S., 33, and Lori L., 32, cling to each other in line, giggling happily. Lori wears a torn T-shirt with the slogan, "Born to be Wild," and tight jeans. Jim is also in jeans, T-shirt and a construction cap. They're eager to tell their story, they say, because for once there is good news to share.

"We moved in with some people who are moving to Missouri in nine days," Lori begins, breathlessly. "We're taking over their house and everything, so we're going from homeless to having a house. Then at the same time, the welfare program gave him a job with a brand new restaurant!"

"It's an Italian restaurant," Jim adds, proudly.

"So we're getting all set," Lori continues. "The next step will be to get my children. With his job and this house I'll be able to get the kids back. They're not with me, because of drugs and alcohol and we were homeless. But we've both been clean, and doing really good. My

daughter's 6 and my son is 7.

"So, why we're here is, we're paying our rent, to help with the house we're living in right now. Then we're gonna take over the rent payments. It's a one bedroom house, $275 a month, but on two acres, a mile from his job. And then," she giggles and squeezes Jim's arm, "we're gonna get married. We're already discussing that."

How did they get to the point of homelessness?

"Well," explains Lori, "I divorced my husband. That was like six years ago, and I haven't even been in a home since. I've just been staying with friends."

"She hooked up with me," Jim continues, "and I told her it was time to get out of this. We started praying, and the past couple weeks have been a real turnaround. A job, a house. It's great."

Lori's only job was at a Jack-in-the-Box restaurant a couple of years ago. Jim last worked a year ago as cook and manager at a restaurant.

"So now I'm gonna be a head chef and shift supervisor for this new restaurant," he says.

Lori's eyes cloud when asked about her job prospects. "I, um, can't work right now," she stammers. "Cause I just, I just, I guess I'm working on my drug ability. I used meth (methamphetamine, or "speed") for so many years. I'm not withdrawing, but I get tired. I was in Narcotics Anonymous for nine months, but I can't get stuck with all that ugly past. They make you look at all the stuff that made you feel bad, like my family and my children. Me, I want to concentrate on getting my children back."

Jim interjects, "We're in self-treatment. I went through the Teen Challenge program, and came that close to being a minister – Pentecostal. With the job and everything, we're gonna get a whole new class of friends, get away from all the bad habits. A new beginning, you know?"

"I hate 'em (drugs) so much," Lori says. "Now I'm going through a dentist thing, 'cause I did drugs and my teeth are all bad. I did drugs since I was 13, and I'm 32 now. I did just a little of everything, but meth, mainly. We were slammin' it. My Mom would do it. My Dad, he's an alky, so it was like, really fun. But not no more. When your family parties, it's real hard to kick it.

"All's I want to do is get my children and settle down. They're with their dad, but he's in a drug program. We want to grab the children and say, 'lookit what's out here'. We both can do it now – stay clean and settle down and everything, so maybe our children can grow up good. I just pray every day my children won't have to go through this whole thing of drugs and alcohol, like my parents and me. My parents are still doing it. And it's like, maybe I can get control of my children before they think, 'hey, Mom and Dad, let me have some!' "

"Yep," says Jim, "It's our own little success story. Finally."

WORKING THE WINDOW

LENA ALEXANDER, 77, WORKED AS A stenographer for the state of California until 1969. She was one of the first Food Bank volunteers.

"I started when they first opened the food locker, way back in '70-something, down in the basement at Immaculate Conception Church, and I've been working there ever since. There were three or four of us working down in the basement, and every fifteen minutes or so, one of us would take a bag upstairs to the people who wanted food. I used to take my knitting with me. We had time to sit around, knit and read, but you never have any of that now. It's grown too much. I marvel at Father Madigan and what he's done.

"Now I work the computer once a week, every Monday from noon till 2:00 or 2:30, checking IDs and filling out the form that says how much food each person needs. They usually close the gate at 2:00, but we keep working until everyone's served.

"Then I work at the Sunday lunch program the first and fifth Sunday of every month. On Sundays, I get there at 10:00, start making sandwiches. At 12:00 the boss, Mario, puts me over on the window. I serve the adults, and my friend Frances Zeitler serves the children. We work the window until 2:00. We're always the last ones to leave, Fran and I.

"The last Sunday of the month is very busy. People have run out of their money by then, and have to wait until the first of the month to get another check. Oh, gosh, we serve 1,800 to 1,900 people lots of times. There are so many more in line now than there were. I think there are more families, and big families. We fix a nice bag lunch: sandwiches, fruit, juice, cookies or cake.

"I haven't had any problems with anybody, working at the window. I think there are people that come to the window that probably don't need to, but how are you going to know? I had a lady come one day that needed food, and I asked her for ID, and she showed me her cable TV bill. I thought, golly, she must not be too bad off. But how do you know? Some of them look like they really, really need it badly. It's awful hard to judge.

"Maybe I'm a little more lenient than a lot of people. I think if they stand in line for a long time, they should be given something. I can remember years ago when Father Madigan said, 'If they push themselves aside to come and beg for food, we can't turn them down.' I've never turned anybody down. I just can't.

"Now we have new rules that say if a person has been there already that month we can only give them bread. I hate doing that. I don't like that part of it, but I guess they have to do it, or they would run out of food. It's just awfully hard to say no.

"There's Mondays when I think, 'Gee, I wish I didn't have to go over there.' But after I do my job, I feel good about it. I feel awfully good when I leave there – like I've really done something."

SUNDAY LUNCH

IT IS 11:30 ON THE THIRD SUNDAY OF THE month, and the line of people stretches from the wrought-iron gate to the Food Bank warehouse and 100 feet down the sidewalk. Mario Stefani, the 76-year-old director of the Sunday Lunch program, walks briskly outside the gate to survey the line. He wears a blue apron over his jeans, and still carries the broom he'd used to sweep the corridor by the Food Bank windows.

"Hey. You name Mario?" asks a heavy, 20ish man in a tight T-shirt and rumpled jeans. Mario nods. "What can I do for you?"

"Can I get one more bag?" the man asks. "Cause the guy in there say you the one makes the rules."

Before Mario can answer affirmatively, he is approached by a woman in her 30s, her head wrapped in a scarf and her legs spindly under a swollen belly. She appears exhausted, wobbly, as if at any moment she will grab the energetic Mario's arm for support.

"It's a real long line," she explains. "And I don't wanna pass out on you guys today like I did last week. I came to get my lunch, but I don't want to stand there. I'm real sick. I have cancer. I have a little girl – it's just me and her."

Stefani promises both he'll be right back, walks into the warehouse corridor and returns with the sack lunches for both the man and the woman.

"Once I was at the window, handing out

the bags, and this gal wanted several bags for her kids," Stefani recalls. "She said they were home sick with the chicken pox. Usually we ask to see the person the lunch is for, and it was just her, so I wouldn't give her the extra bags. Well, she left and returned with her sick kids,

all blotchy with chicken pox. Did I feel horrible! So now, whatever they say, I go ahead and give it to them – up to a point."

The corridor alongside the Food Bank windows is, as usual, cacophonous.

"Ray-NEE!" screams a woman.

"I got three kids, man," a man shouts at the volunteer behind the window. "They's outside. Damn!"

"Don't you kids go nowhere. RAY-NEEE!"

Mary N., a 29-year-old mother of three, says Sunday Lunch is a happy ritual for her young family.

"We live in those apartments right down there," she says, pointing to a dilapidated building down the street from the Food Bank, "and everybody in those apartments is poor. So Sundays, the kids just love it. It's, 'Let's go, mom! I wanna get my lunch!' They come down here, get lunch, they all

sit around and have like a little picnic and it really makes it nice. Because every kid has one. I always feel bad, because I go to make my son something, and he says, 'Mom, my friend wants something! He hasn't eaten.' And I have to say, 'Well, son, I don't have enough.'

"This is nice, because the kids can do it as a group thing. We all come down, we all get our lunch, we all go back to the apartments, everyone sits around."

Inside the warehouse, 20 volunteers form a sandwich-making, cookie bagging, fruit sorting, sack dispensing assembly line. Spatulas slap "goop" the Sunday Lunch program's "secret sauce" – onto hundreds of slices of wheat bread. The wheat bread has seen fresher days, but moldy pieces are discarded. Fresh ham and cheese slices are added after the goop.

"I won't work the window," confesses volunteer Margaret Bullock, spreading goop at dizzying speed. "They're not happy people," she asserts. Bullock, 42, is a state worker who volunteers one Sunday a month with her aunt, retired preschool director Lee Salerno. The aunt slaps ham and cheese between the slices of sauced bread.

Salerno sighs. "All those people with bags in their shopping carts. They gotta do something. There's too many of them. So many of them aren't well."

Down the table, elderly Lucy Buljan stoops over a ten-pound box of pink and chocolate cookies, repackaging them by handfuls into small baggies. Buljan has been working Sundays for Father Madigan's charities for nearly 20 years, beginning with

cooking and serving hot meals in the auditorium across the street at Immaculate Conception Church.

"You can't say no to Father Madigan," she says with a chuckle. "And it seems like there's more people that need help nowadays." So even though she's too frail to drive a car, Buljan comes every Sunday with a friend to make lunches for the needy.

White-haired, cheerful Joe Ostoja, another veteran volunteer, wanders in from the hallway and shouts an announcement: "Good news! There's a double line all the way up here, so don't run outta gas. We need you here for a good hour and a half more!" It is 12:30.

Joe goes back down the hall to a windowless room equipped with double freezers, industrial sized meat slicer and sinks. Three more "old-timers" are there, talking, slicing and concocting the sandwich goop.

Ed DeWinter, a trim retired Army sergeant major who still wears a buzz cut, slices massive piles of ham as the three chat about the old days at the Food Bank.

Fifteen years ago the same three friends were stirring spaghetti and other hot meals in the basement of Immaculate Conception church, serving it with baked goods made by their wives. When the crowds grew too big to handle, Father Madigan began a fundraising drive to purchase the abandoned Arata Bros. grocery warehouse complex that now houses SFBS and its Oak Park food locker.

"That was about six years ago," recalls DeWinter. "It took us about a year to settle on whether we should have a sit-down meal. What Father wanted to figure out here was, how can we feed more people? I told him, if you have a sit-down dinner, you're not going to feed as many people as if you have a bag meal. Give them a bag and away they go. You'd need three times the volunteers with a sit-down meal, plus you'd have problems with health and sanitation. Here, the only thing you have to concern yourself with is keeping your slicers clean."

The men had started with 90 pounds of cheese that morning and had already run out. Each Sunday they slice at least 200 pounds of meat, bought by Stefani at a discount for 35 cents a pound.

Don Rund, 60 and a retired refueling systems operator from Mather Air Force Base, reveals the secret of his sandwich sauce: "It's whatever I can find, from mayonnaise to thousand island, Worcestershire, whatever. We mix it up, and it tastes good."

Ostoja, who's been working Sundays for 15 years, says he misses Sunday football on TV. Even though for years he's been talking about taking a "sabbatical" on the recliner watching the 49ers, he concedes he'll probably put in another year anyway.

"You gotta remember Father Madigan," he says. "Father Madigan is the Will Rogers of the priesthood. Remember Will Rogers was such a likeable man, everybody loved him and even wanted him to run for President of the United States? Madigan affects people the same way.

"Sure, we're here because of what we're doing, too. But you gotta have a good quarterback."

Victoria and Ursula Ramirez, wearing Easter dresses from the Clothes Closet

CLOTHING THE POOR

THE CLOTHES CLOSET

APRIL 1985

Dear Friends:

It is easy to be nice to those who send us thank you cards, shake our hand and tell us how helpful we have been. These are usually our family members, friends and neighbors, co-workers perhaps – all people of our own kind.

It's not so easy to be nice to the ungrateful, the boring or burdensome, the winos and bums, the embarrassingly down-at-the-heel panhandlers, or others below us on the scale of "class." And yet these are the ones to whom the Lord told us to be nice. "What you do to the *least* of My brothers, you do to Me." Nowhere did He say what we do for the prosperous and popular we do for Him. It is in the weak, the sick, the sinners, the losers, specifically in *them* He told us to look for Him and serve Him. And so, in late evening when the rectory door bell sends me down the stairs to look through the peephole, I know I am going to have a choice to make. When I see that a man on the porch is not a parishioner but a shabby, disheveled street person, I can do one of two things. I can tiptoe back up the stairs, pretending no one is home, and my visitor will soon walk away. On the other hand, if I open the door, street people are never the most appealing to deal with. They wear a hodge-podge of odds and ends fished from trash bins and often they reek of cheap booze, sweat and urine. They rarely express themselves well and their awkward speech and manners vary from servility to rudeness. Yet here waits a human being in need of almost everything – a bath, clean clothes, food, a place to sleep and, most of all, an encouraging word. It would be so easy to pretend I'm out.

Choice stares me in the face. In all honesty, I must say that when I open the door, which I do, it is more often than not a real act of faith, blind trust that Jesus meant what He said about finding Him in this specific "least" brother. It is hard sometimes to see Him in eyes haunted by rejections, fears, suspicions, even hatreds. But I know that I must try.

May the Good Lord bless you,

Fr. Dan Madigan

Dear Friends:

Poverty is on the increase nationwide. Locally, it's booming, according to our own food locker figures. In 1976, 2,700 people came to us in person seeking food, whereas last year, 1988, 140,809 people came with the same need.

Only a mellow and flexible person is able to work at the distribution window and successfully interact with the many different individuals. A high level of charity, kindness and patience is imperative for the job, as volunteers quickly learn. After all, clients bring their personalities as well as their problems to the window. Some are crude. Some are hostile. Some try to lie and cheat. But the vast majority are very kind, receptive and extremely grateful for the help they are receiving.

Because of you, I feel we have climbed two mountains of need. With you, our donors and volunteers, we now feed and clothe the poor and we do it well. Our 12,000 square-foot clothing outlet is the result of years of experimentation. It now runs smoothly, benefiting families and singles alike. But there are more mountains to conquer. We are eyeing these in the hope of successfully taking on their challenges, with the Good Lord's never-failing help.

Above all, we ask for your prayers, that God will show us clearly what needs to be done and inspire us with the way to go about it.

With every good wish,

Fr. Dan Madigan

Dear Friends:

What is needed today is straight forward talk like the early church got from St. John Chrysostom (344-407). Today Chrysostom needs to return and tell both Church and State that it's their people that are important and not all the other things they so often put ahead of them.

Many centuries ago St. John Chrysostom said: "Would you honor Christ here in church clothed in silk vestments and then pass Him by unclothed and frozen outside? We must learn to be discerning Christians and to honor Christ in the way in which He wants to be honored. God has no need of golden vessels but of golden hearts.

"I am not saying you should not give golden altar vessels, but I am insisting that nothing can take the place of almsgiving. The gift of a chalice may be ostentatious; almsgiving is pure benevolence. What is the use of loading Christ's table with gold cups while He Himself is starving? Feed the hungry and then if you have any money left over, spend it on the altar table. Will you make a cup of gold and withhold a cup of water? What use is it to adorn the altar with cloth of gold hangings and deny Christ a coat for His back!

"Tell me: If you saw someone starving and refused to give him any food but instead spent your money on adorning the altar with gold, would Christ thank you? Would He not instead be outraged? Or if you saw someone in rags and stiff with cold and then did not give him clothing but set up golden columns in Christ's honor, would He not say He was being made a fool of and insulted?"

Friends, how wise this great man was. Would to God that our thinking was as clear as his.

With every best wish to you,

Fr. Dan Madigan

Dear Friends:

Saint Basil was born in Cappadocia in 330. Serving as Bishop of Caesarea, he died in 379. He was no diplomat. He explained the gospel the way he understood it. He said: "The bread in your box belongs to the hungry; the cloak in your closet belongs to the naked; the shoes you do not wear belong to the barefoot; the money in your vault belongs to the destitute."

An old friend once asked Henry Ford, "Why don't you ever buy any nuts and bolts from me?" Mr. Ford replied, "Heck, Joe, you never asked me."

I myself fall somewhere between Saint Basil and Henry Ford's friend. I am not as strong as one or as shy as the other. I do ask. And ask often. And, yes, I do receive.

August is always a demanding month by way of requests for help. Our statistics bear this out. The reason for the increase is the added expense on parents of procuring clothing for children returning to school.

You, my friends, are givers. I am the recipient of your charity. I promise you I will try to get the best possible mileage and the greatest amount of good out of your contributions to us.

May God bless you for your inner kindness.

Fr. Dan Madigan

CHARITY WITH DIGNITY

PEOPLE TAKE UP THE CAUSE OF FOOD, of

literacy and homelessness, but the need for clothing the poor

never attracts much publicity. Yet when we look at graphs of services

we provide over the year, what month do you suppose is the toughest for

poor families? It is August, the month when parents are struggling to buy school

clothes and at the same time feed their families on limited incomes.

Whether they're on welfare, in minimum wage or seasonal jobs, food and rent eat up their

entire budget.

A politician I respect, former Assemblyman Phil Isenberg of Sacramento, says govern-

ment agencies "frequently measure success by the amount of money in their budgets, not

whether they are succeeding at anything." That's something we charities should consider, when examining what it takes to make a program work.

The Clothes Closet at SFBS is an example of an enormously practical service rendered with a tiny budget. There's very little glorification that goes along with it. Certainly no one would fund you for a Clothes Closet. But just watching the people in our food lines convinced us there was a great need for one here. Many were without coats on cold winter days. Children wore ill-fitting pants and walked with holes in their shoes, while their mothers tried to dress up shabby outfits with a colorful scarf or belt. Many looked as if they'd given up – their stained, tattered clothing advertised despair.

Of course, many well-meaning churches and neighborhood centers have clothing "boxes" – rumpled sweaters, slacks and undergarments of all sizes, carelessly jumbled together so that the poor may dive in and scrounge for scraps. Others have established self-supporting or profit-making thrift stores, where the poor may pay less than retail for clothes that are less than new. Middle-class people go to regular stores and buy new clothes. Poor people go to thrift shops. But what about the destitute, who don't have even a dollar for a dress?

As we recognized the need for clean, well cared-for clothing to be generously given away, we also realized a need for a system of organization to allow us to do this with dignity. Two incidents impressed this upon me. The first occurred some years ago, when we were first running our soup kitchen out of the Immaculate Conception Church basement. A local minister had, through some connection in Los Angeles, been offered an entire truck load of new clothing – he only had to rent a truck, drive down and pick it up. We helped with the truck rental, and drove what must have been $200,000 worth of new clothing to our Catholic elementary school in Oak Park, where the clothes were put up on hangers to be given away. There was enough, it seemed, to have clothed every poor person in the neighborhood for a year. All this clothing was delivered to the minister's church, and his staff handled the distribution. I gave him the idea of distributing it systematically, as we distributed food in our lockers. Unfortunately, his staff set up no clear guidelines to prevent anyone from taking undue advantage. Without such a system, there was no way to ensure that the supply would last to provide the most benefit to the most people. Within a matter of weeks, all the clothing was gone.

The second incident was after the Loma Prieta Earthquake, when John Healey and I drove a truckload of food and clothing to the stricken community of Watsonville. Once we arrived, it became clear that emergency officials didn't need any more food or clothing – mountains of canned goods and donated clothing had already arrived. What was needed was a disciplined distribution system to bring the goods to those in the most need. I returned from that experience convinced that *how* goods are distributed can be as important as *what* is available to distribute. It's the same with food as with clothing. If you put something out and don't supervise its distribution, you bring out the worst in people, and that's not fair. It's not fair to them, because they're poor, they need it, and they're trying to get as much as they can. Their intentions are good. But without some order, such a give-away becomes a demeaning experience.

With those thoughts in mind, our Clothes Closet has developed a dignified system that relies on countless volunteer hours of manual labor, but very little in the way of costly overhead. We try to run the outlet as much as possible like a store where families might browse quietly for what they need. Only ten people are allowed to "shop" at a time, so never is there a "free-for-all" atmosphere. All our clothing is clean, pressed, on hangers and arranged by size for men, women, and children. Accessories and shoes are attractively displayed. Shelves of items such as blankets, pillows and fabric remnants are also available. Much of the clothing we receive is absolutely immaculate. Many business people will go so far as to send their clothes to the dry cleaners, and bring them in starched and bagged.

When we opened the doors of the clothes closet in 1988, we had no need for advertising. People who lined up for food soon were lining up for clothing. Today, we distribute more than 1,000 pieces of clothing a day, and it's done in a dignified, organized way. In addition, we collect and set aside cloth-ing for uniforms for low-income students at two neighborhood schools, and business outfits for clients who need suitable cloth-ing for job interviews.

The people who work in the clothing out-let have to be extremely sensitive to donors as well as the clients who come for cloth-ing. Many times a donor has just gotten himself together to bring in the wardrobe of a late spouse, and the volunteer is meet-ing this person on what must be one of the worst days of his life. It's an enormously emotional thing.

One particular donation we received really showed how naive we sometimes are. It was a whole load of surplus jackets from the state government – lovely, warm, woolen jackets. I thought people would snap them right up, but nobody would touch them. It turned out they were from Folsom prison, and everyone in the neighborhood, except old Dan Madigan who's been around forever, recognized them.

That was a little lesson. People may be poor, they may have had brushes with the law, but nobody wants to wear that badge.

THE CLOTHES CLOSET

PENNY C., A MIDDLE-AGED MOTHER OF THREE teenagers, hands a paper slip marked with the number "8" to the volunteer at the clothing closet desk. She'd arrived when the Clothes Closet doors opened at 10 a.m., hoping to get her turn to shop the boys' and men's racks early. Still, there were seven people ahead of her, some having waited nearly two hours. Penny, her unemployed husband and three teens live in a motel room that costs $575 a month. It includes a refrigerator and stove, she says, "but every time I put the stove on, it blows the circuit breakers." The family's monthly welfare check is $723, leaving $148 to feed, clothe, bathe and transport five adult-sized people. The inadequate kitchen facilities make it hard for Penny to save money cooking. Most of the family's meals are sandwiches.

"So, I hit the food lockers, and I hit the clothes closets for them," Penny says with a shrug and resigned smile.

Clothes Closet director Margaret Carpenter, energetic, intense, superbly organized, asks Penny some particulars, retrieves a card with Penny's name and address from a set of boxed files, and hands her a large box for the clothing she may choose.

On a wall opposite the desk where Margaret takes numbers are lists that explicitly detail how many and what sort of items each customer may take. Men, 16 years and older, are entitled to one each of the following: dress shirts, T-shirts or knit shirts, dress slacks, jeans or work slacks, sweat pants, dress jacket, sweater, shoes, robe or pajamas, cap, hat or gloves, scarf, neckties, belts. They may choose two pairs of shorts and two sets of underwear.

Women, aged 16 and older, are entitled to a greater number and variety of items, because more women's clothes are donated. Each customer may choose one each: dress, two-piece suit, jeans, sweat pants, sweat shirts, shoes, slippers, robe, pajamas, bra, slip, purse, hat or gloves, scarf. Customers may choose two of the following: skirts, T-shirts, sweaters, shorts, belts; and four each of dress slacks, shirts or blouses.

Under the front desk, there are ten boxes like the one Margaret has handed Penny. When customers are finished shopping, their choices are marked on a list by Margaret or another volunteer, and transferred to a bag. The box is then available for another customer, and Margaret calls another number.

Penny searches the racks for slacks for her 15- and 16-year-old boys. They need them, she said, because "they both want back in school." The younger one had gotten into trouble, she said, and was just released from a four-month sentence in Juvenile Hall. His older brother hadn't been in school since his brother's arrest led to the family's eviction and move to a motel on the other side of the county. Both have four full years of high school ahead of them.

Penny's husband, who's had on-and-off jobs as a security guard, is hoping to get training as an air conditioning and refrigeration repairman, through the county's Greater Avenues to Independence (GAIN) program, she said. But in order to qualify, he, too, needs a high school diploma.

Penny has an appointment the next day with school district officials to talk about getting her boys back on track. Meanwhile, with her slightly used pairs of jeans and sweaters in a plastic bag, she plans to walk downtown – a distance of about four miles – to another charity where lunch is served. Penny says she relies on SFBS' Clothes Closet and Food Locker, particularly at the end of the month, when the welfare check has run out.

"The people are courteous here," she says. "The Clothes Closet is bigger than any others, and you can pick different things for your kids. My kids need jeans more than anything, so I got them jeans and a few shorts. They'll be happy with that."

As Penny begins her walk, a younger mother, Mary M., hands her number to Margaret, then chases after her year-and-a-half-old daughter, who has escaped under the racks of clothing. Mary's three-year-old daughter is busy thumbing through a children's book on a chair by the Clothes Closet entrance. The active toddler cuts Mary's visit short, but she manages to find some children's clothes, a shirt for her six-year-old son, a blouse and socks for herself. She walks outside with a friend, Sharon, who's found a new skirt and T-shirt for herself.

Mary and Sharon are friends from the neighborhood, and are bound by the common problems of poverty. Both are on welfare – Mary gets Aid to Families with Dependent Children, and Sharon, $200 a month in county General Assistance payments. Mary struggles to be a loving and effective mother despite her tight finances. Her husband is good to her and the kids, she says, although his employment as a mechanic and auto refurbisher is sporadic. However poor the family may be, she says she is determined it will not disintegrate in the manner of her own childhood family.

"We always had a really beautiful home when I was a little girl," Mary says. "My mom and dad were together, and my dad was in the Air Force. We always had beautiful Christmases — I can remember that long table with the big chairs. And then my mom divorced my dad and my dad left, and everything fell apart. My mom couldn't cope raising eight kids, and she started drinking. I'd move from foster home to foster home, and was abused in some. Finally I ran away from the system when I was 14."

She never finished high school but worked to support herself from age 16, and became a mother herself at 18. When that child was three, Mary gave her up for adoption.

"I just couldn't do it," she recalls. "I couldn't put her through what I had gone through. So I told my family I would put her up for adoption so she can grow up with a mom and dad. I love her with all my heart, and I tried and I tried and couldn't do it. She was three when I gave her up. I even attempted suicide because I got to the point where I just felt I wasn't being a good enough mom. I had slit my wrist, and I was crying to my sister, 'Am I a good mom?'

"You know what my sister said, then? She said, 'You're not a BAD mom, but you're a poor mom, and you're in the system, and you'll never get out of the system.'" She is silent a moment, staring somewhere in the distance. Then, as if snapping to attention, she says crisply, "Well, my daughter has a good family now. And we're keeping our family together, too."

A thin woman with lank blonde hair pulled back into a pony tail, Mary smiles to reveal teeth long in need of a dentist. She says she hopes to one day get out of "the system" by training to be a nurse. But for now, she must volunteer 20 hours a week or find employment in order to continue receiving welfare benefits.

Her friend, Sharon, is dressed for job-hunting: black checked skirt and black sweater, makeup, nail polish and a handbag to match her black flats. She looks the part of an office worker on lunch break, but her life at the moment includes neither jobs nor breaks.

"I gotta find something," she says. "Even if it's cleaning toilets, but I'd hate to." A graduate of high school who was close to finishing beauty college before a drug-dealing boyfriend convinced her to quit and stay home with their child, she's recently been released from a 41-day jail sentence for drunk driving. She says she has lost custody of her two children, been evicted from her apartment, and had half her clothes stolen by somebody at the last house in which she stayed.

"And last night, someone stole my bike," she adds, shaking her head with a wry smile. "Can you believe it?"

"I wanna get out of this scene — away from the drugs and everything, or I'll never get my kids back. And since I don't have my kids, I can't get my homeless (county benefits that help pay rental deposits). Without a place, it's really hard to find a job, because you need an address, a phone, something."

"It's hard out there," Mary interjects sympathetically. "I keep telling her, 'Come stay on my floor.' At least she'll be safe." Sharon says she might take Mary up on the offer. For now, they'll take the Clothes Closet items back to Mary's place, and Sharon will start making phone calls.

Inside, Margaret passes a box to number 27, a gaunt Laotian man with a palsied face who is dressed for freezing weather despite Indian summer temperatures. He chooses three jackets from the racks, and is told he must choose just one among them. Bewildered, he holds all three out to the volunteer.

"I'm sorry, only one," she says, holding up a finger. He nods, then decides on the warmest, but not the nicest, of the three, a fiber-filled ski parka.

Margaret, who worked in a nursery for 20 years before volunteering, then taking a full time job directing the Clothes Closet, starts each day sorting clothes at 7:45 a.m. She is on her feet until 4 p.m., sorting, directing, straightening, filling out forms.

In a room behind the clothing "store," a half-dozen volunteers sort through a seemingly bottomless bin of donated clothing, putting aside soiled items to be taken home and laundered, tossing torn pieces into a bag for recycling, hanging up and organizing the best. Volunteer Nellie Mackie sorts through baby clothes to create layettes for expectant mothers.

"What this originally started out with, back in 1991, was just enough to bring a baby home from the hospital," she explains. "The hospitals were calling here, saying mothers were going to the hospital with nothing.

"At that time, we hardly had any baby clothes. All I had to give was a plastic bag with a couple of scroungy little shirts, sleepers that sagged. Now, the word is out and we have plenty." She shows off a wrapped layette: a hand-knit blanket, cotton receiving blanket, hooded towel, lap pad, nightgown, sleepers, two tee-shirts, two cloth diapers and an infant's disposable diaper.

Around five expectant mothers come each week for Mackie's layettes. They return after the baby is born to fill out the wardrobe.

Each day, Margaret puts several coats on the rack, always holding some back for the next day's customers. In a separate room, she reserves the nicest outfits for men and women who have job interviews: business suits, accessorized skirts and dresses with matching shoes and handbags. A box is filled with tiny white patent leather shoes and purses, in preparation for next Easter or a little girl's communion.

"You don't realize how it is until you start working here," says Margaret. "How many people are homeless and how many people are needing clothes. I never knew this.

"What really makes me feel good is when customers come back and donate their clothes, after they've gotten a job. They'll say, 'You were there and helped me, now it's my turn.' And when you give somebody a coat and see that big smile? When people say, 'Thank you, God bless you,' that's when I feel the best."

Audrey and her tutor, Don

PROVIDING TOOLS

READING PROGRAM

JANUARY 1990

Dear Friends:

We commonly think that study is the road to learning. But continued study alone will eventually only paralyze a mind. The person who really wishes to learn must not only study but also apply the knowledge gained to practical uses. Somehow one must give back what one gets or one will lose what one gets.

I believe that the law of life is that nothing can come into us unless it can get out of us. The Dead Sea has an inlet but no outlet. Its water level is maintained by evaporation. I believe that's what also happens to knowledge that is not used. It evaporates.

Electricity, on the other hand, has an inlet and an outlet. Power runs through its wire. And so it must be with us. God's love is meant to travel through us to others.

We just cannot become a Dead Sea. We cannot stagnate. There's lots of work to be done. Please give me a call. Step forward, volunteer and join our team.

With every good wish to you and yours,

Fr. Dan Madigan

My Dear Friends:

It's heartwarming to see people travel from poverty to prosperity. It's sad to see them slide from comfort to destitution. The Talmud puts it well when it says, "Life is a wheel – he who is on top today may be on the bottom tomorrow."

Ronald Reagan's great-grandfather was born in Ireland in a bogland area called Doolis, near the town of Ballyporeen, in the County of Tipperary. Here is a journalist's description of a visit paid in those days to the Reagan ancestral neighborhood:

"A starved-looking and half-naked old woman, barefooted and shivering with age and pain, besought me to see her cabin in Doolis. The unfortunate creature had built it herself of sod and stones, and thatched it with heather and rushes. The approaches to it were swimming with liquid manure and mud; the odors around the place were revolting. A coarse platter of yellow stirabout without even salt represented the whole food of the establishment and an iron pot the entire furniture."

It's no wonder that the Reagan family left there. Ireland with its hunger, turmoil and oppression was too cruel for them. The New World with its freedom, hope and opportunity turned their wheel of life around.

My family, my teachers, the Church and the USA all helped in turning my wheel of life to where it is today. I hope I will never forget that. I hope too that I will never lose sight of Shakespeare's advice "not to scorn the steps by which we ascend the ladder of life."

Because of your supportive empathy we do help people turn their wheel of life around. We feed them – we clothe them – we befriend them – we educate them. We let them know they are beautiful and important.

Thank you for your wonderful kindness to the poor. May God truly bless you for your kind heart.

With every good wish to you,

Fr. Dan Madigan

Dear Friends:

Millions of European immigrants came to the U.S.A. in the mid-1800's. They came in search of a new life. They often left behind them severe hunger, turmoil and oppression. Here is the story of one of them.

Pat sailed into New York harbor. He received immediate consolation from the beautiful words on the Statue of Liberty.

"Give me your tired, your poor, your huddled masses yearning to breathe free."

After being processed at Ellis Island, Pat went into a cafeteria in New York City to get something to eat. He sat down at an empty table and waited for someone to take his order. Nobody did. Finally, a man with a tray full of food sat down opposite him and told him how things worked.

"Start at that end," he said, "and just go along and pick out what you want. At the other end they'll tell you how much you have to pay for it."

Pat quickly learned that American life is cafeteria style.

Here at Sacramento Food Bank Services we feed, clothe, house, educate, and provide mother-baby care to hurting families.

And we go a further step. We show people that American life is truly cafeteria style. We teach folks that they can get things provided they pay for them. We teach them that no one will bring them stuff. They have to get up and scrounge for themselves.

Please join our SFBS team in promoting this philosophy of self-actualization.

We know that all people have wings. We know that all people can fly. But what we so often forget is that all of us had to have support, company and companionship when we went on our maiden voyages.

God bless you – take care of yourselves.

Fr. Dan Madigan

Dear Friends:

I am well acquainted with Oak Park's illiteracy. For 13 years (1976-89), I ran this district's only grade school. Seventy percent of our children were minorities. Many came from very chaotic homes. Yet practically all our graduates went on to high school. Many even to college.

We attributed our success to strong emphasis on family values. Self-discipline. Good study habits. Homework. Close working relationship with parents. Strong leadership and dedicated volunteers.

At our Sacramento Reading Center, SFBS works with adults who had few of those advantages. Many have been passed through overcrowded school classrooms, learning little but a sense of frustration and failure. Those adults who have courageously come through our doors are seeking help to regain the solid foothold of education. In an atmosphere of respect and support, they also gain self-esteem.

The students hungry enough to show up week after week for tutoring learn a whole world is open to them with mastery of the written word. Job applications, newspapers and books are no longer viewed as frightening obstacles but as tools for self-empowerment.

Most of the 60 reading center tutors have been raised with the values we tried to instill at our elementary school. It takes extraordinary patience, at times, to stick through the learning process with adults who haven't had those advantages. The rewards, when they appear, are intangible: a smile of recognition, signs of growing confidence, a diploma achieved.

It is person-to-person contact that makes a difference. Students who struggled and gave up in large classrooms find in our Reading Center an atmosphere where they can thrive – at their own pace, without competition or harsh judgment. There are no handouts at the Reading Center, but there are plenty of hands to hold.

Take care of yourselves. And if you are a person who has been taught self-discipline, good communication skills, literacy and strong values, thank God once again.

With every good wish,

Fr. Dan Madigan

F A C I N G I L L I T E R A C Y

I CAME OUT OF A CULTURE IN IRELAND where

even the poor were educated. I saw a lot of shortage, but never

deep poverty. There were probably one or two very old people in the

village who were considered illiterate, but they'd have some knowledge of

math and simple words. As for the younger generations, no matter how poor people

were, everyone went to school.

When I first came to this country and was stationed in Del Paso Heights, there was a fairly

large group of people in the neighborhood who decided to join the Catholic Church. Many of

them were black, and most of them were drawn to us through their kids, who found in the

church a place they could socialize. On a couple of occasions a year I would take busloads of up

to 80 kids to a big camp the Catholic diocese had in the mountains.

We'd enjoy the outdoors and at night sit and watch movies or play games. It was a big adventure for these kids, and they were amazingly well-behaved.

Soon, a whole group of their parents and neighbors expressed interest in joining the church, and I decided I would give them a very intense course in Catholicism. Now, I came out of a system where we were lectured to, never given the opportunity to ask questions, and there was no such thing as class participation. So with this class in Del Paso Heights, I followed the only method I knew. I lectured to them, and there was no class participation.

There was one tiny woman in this class I often wondered about. I wondered if she wasn't that bright, or wasn't understanding the lectures, but because of the way the class was run, I really had nothing to verify my feelings.

At the end of this six-month course, I gave the class an examination. It was a true-or-false exam of 100 questions, some of which were my own, and some which I gleaned from religious textbooks. It was a tough, tough examination. You'd really have to know your stuff to do well, I thought.

I graded each exam, then interviewed each person in the class individually. When I came to this woman's exam, I found she did about 50-50: half right, half wrong. Which wasn't too bad, as far as I was concerned, considering the difficulty of the exam. In front of each question I had put a "T" and an "F", for true and false, and asked them to circle the appropriate one.

I noticed that this woman had made little markings all over her paper. It seemed she had drawn a line under every "T" and every "F" in each sentence.

When I sat down and talked to her, I found out that this woman was not able to read. Even so, she had believed she was capable of coming in and taking that examination. She believed she knew how to do it. Apparently she knew how to count, and she recognized letters – at least she had taught herself "T" and "F." So for each question, she counted the number of "T"s in the sentence, and counted the "F"s. Whichever was the "winner," meaning whichever letter appeared most often, was the one she put down for her answer.

I recall this story to remind myself how out of touch I was, how bureaucratic I was and, in retrospect, how naive. How far removed and how ill-prepared I was for dealing with true poverty, which is poverty of the mind as well as the pocketbook.

Around that same time, in the late 1960s, I was given another reminder. I decided it would be a good idea to start a men's group at the church. There was tremendous response to this idea – maybe 30 men showed up. At the first meeting, I appointed myself chairman. That wasn't very democratic, but I felt I had maybe a bit more skill and education than the people that were there, and that I could help the organization get off the ground. At the end of six months, it was time for the men to elect their own leaders. So the men nominated some officers, and at the next meeting they were to elect leaders from among their nominees, using written ballots.

At the next meeting, when they were to mark the ballots, I got a very poor response. A number of the men did not show up to vote. I got very down about it. Being young and enthusiastic I personalized it, and felt that these particular men had let me down.

I went to talk things over with Frank, one of the men in the club. He was a blue-collar worker with about ten little kids, very outgoing and apparently successful in his work. I said, "Frank, I was very disappointed in this election. I feel you guys let me down."

Frank said simply, "Well, I can tell you why I was not there, and I think I can tell you why the others weren't there. We can't read and write."

I was flabbergasted. Here was a whole group of grown men who could not even read a man's name on a piece of paper.

When I moved to Oak Park, one of my duties as pastor was directing the Catholic school, which was the only elementary school in this troubled neighborhood. Seventy percent of our student body was minority, many were non-Catholic, and virtually all were poor.

I worked closely with our students in Oak Park, proudly watching them graduate and keeping track of many of them as they went on to high school and college. I firmly believed in the Vatican II appeal to pastors and people to "spare no sacrifice...in helping Catholic schools achieve their purpose" in showing special concern for the poor and in reaching out to non-Catholics and all minorities.

We did have many brilliant successes at the school, and some of our students went on to

achieve degrees from top universities. But it was often a struggle to teach literacy, values, and morals in a neighborhood plagued with crime and troubled families. I remember vividly the time our principal walked two "problem students" home, aiming to talk to their mother about their dismal grades and behavior. When the mother answered the door at 2:00 that afternoon, she was wrapped in a negligee. She listened to the principal's concerns, until a man's voice from a back bedroom interrupted. "Get back in here," he said. "That's not what I'm paying you for."

That ugly story has served as a reminder that, as important as education is, a person's mind cannot be receptive to learning unless the basic needs of the body and soul are also met.

Later on, after we started SFBS, we opened a Reading Center with the idea of bringing educational opportunity to adults who had lost out as children. If we could reach illiterate parents, we felt, surely their children would benefit.

SCENES FROM THE SACRAMENTO READING CENTER

THE SQUAT, BRICK BUILDING ACROSS THE STREET from the food lines looks from the street like the old-fashioned medical office it once was. But inside the Sacramento Reading Center, it sounds like Babel. Adults chattering in eight different languages crowd into a cramped classroom in the back of the building, squeezing into school desks and squinting at the blackboard.

"When is Independence Day?" asks Sandy Calderon-Carlson, a teacher of English as a Second Language (ESL) from the Sacramento City Unified School District. As she points to the question written on the board, there is fervent whispering in Vietnamese, Russian, Iranian, Spanish, Hmong, Mien and Chinese.

"In-dee-pence?" asks Irina, a bold, bulky woman who wears a beehive hairstyle and blue costume jewelry. She shrugs, palms upward in the air.

Sandy repeats the question, and calls on a Vietnamese woman who covers her mouth with a hand and giggles. "Fourth of July," she says.

"Right! In-de-pen-dence Day is (she writes) the fourth of July, or July 4."

As the class continues, Nguyen, from Vietnam, asks Irina, from Ukraine, what she is wearing on her head. Valery, from Russia, asks Chong, from the Mien tribe in Laos, to please stand up. But most of the class' emphasis is on American customs and citizenship skills, because many of the students are preparing to take citizenship exams.

Down a narrow hallway, doors to tiny rooms once used for medical exams are closed to the sounds of Sandy's class. Inside the windowless rooms, adult students are learning one-on-one with tutors how to "sound it out," how to punctuate or write paragraphs. In a larger room equipped with seven computers, a young woman in a wheelchair writes to an on-line pen pal. She comes to the Reading Center every day on a bus specially equipped for her wheelchair. She returns not only for typing lessons, but because this is where she feels welcomed

and at home.

At the front of the building, in what was once a patients' waiting room, donated sets of Funk & Wagnall's Encyclopedias fill shelves topped with artificial plants. Nine Laotian women crowd around a table on folding chairs. Tutor Ann Hickey, a retired nurse, points to an easel-style blackboard where the words "tall" and "high" are written, and asks her students to use each word in a sentence.

Across the hall, the Reading Center's front office is nearly filled by a copy machine and desk. Here program director Craig Usher, 27, fields calls from timid prospective students, schedules tutors, gives pep talks, pores over reading workbooks and squeezes more students into tinier spaces.

Idealism seems prerequisite for a job in which chaos is frequent, clients lack social skills, there is never enough money, and heartbreaking stories are the norm. Usher is idealistic, diplomatic, wry.

He has accepted the frustrations that come with the territory, "things like, a lot of our students never learned basics such as picking up the phone and calling when you can't keep an appointment," he says.

His job, as he describes it, is "to react to the next person who walks in the door." That person could be a teenaged mother required to study for the Graduation Equivalency Diploma exam or risk losing welfare benefits for her child. It could be a 25-year-old Hispanic construction worker who manages to support a family of five despite frequent bouts of unemployment. Or a refugee from the Mien hill tribe of Laos, raised to adulthood with no written language skills, and now struggling to learn literacy in a foreign language.

A year ago, half of the center's foreign students were of Mexican origin and nearly half were Mien. Lately, Russians have been coming, bringing cousins and neighbors and acquaintances met in the food line or in the Mother-Baby program.

Most of the students are not recent immigrants, but American-born adults who somehow fell through the cracks of the public school system. Many, like 23-year-old Anna S., struggled without notice in crowded inner-city school classrooms, falling irretrievably behind and dropping out of high school. Anna is sharp and articulate, with a sophisticated vocabulary, but has trouble keeping up in classrooms where most teaching is done orally or from notes on a blackboard. She dropped out of school in the tenth grade with a fifth grade reading level. Now, working with a tutor who is a retired dentist, Anna says she is about a year away from getting her GED and starting classes at the local junior college.

Students who don't need English language classes meet twice a week in private, hour-and-a-half sessions with volunteer tutors at the Reading Center. Here the tutors and their students learn to work together at a pace that works for the students. It is also in these sessions that bridges are built between the privileged and disadvantaged, and both learn in the process.

Usher assesses each student on the first visit, and draws up a curriculum using materials designed for teaching literacy to adults. He tries to choose workbooks that cover issues relevant to the student – parenting or job skills, for example.

Since Usher moved from his job operating the Food Locker to run the Reading Center in September, 1994, the program has grown from 29 students to 125. The budget for materials has grown at a much slower pace, from $180 to $350 per month. That means the office's aging copier runs almost constantly, and students often can't take materials home.

"The biggest issue most of our students have when they walk in here is lack of confidence," Usher says. "They come in here almost huddled into a ball, because for their entire lives they've been put down, neglected, or abused."

Many have learning disabilities but were passed along in school until their own sense of failure and frustration caused them to drop out. Their only educational option as adults has been "an adult simulation of the same high school experience that failed them in the first place," Usher says. At the Reading Center, many such students are given their first chance to learn at their own pace and with a style that helps them succeed. Students baffled in large classes where learning is done by taking notes from lectures may progress rapidly if encouraged to read aloud in a private room with a tutor.

Just as exciting for Usher is the education volunteer tutors get as they develop relationships with their disadvantaged students.

He describes Jennifer, a young, white, single professional woman, "looking for something meaningful in her life," who volunteered as a mentor and was paired with Alberta, a young African-American mother who didn't finish high school.

"Jennifer will never again look at a grouping of people such as 'single black moms,' and paint them with the same brush," Usher says. "It can't happen, because through Alberta they've been humanized. I've seen it happen again and again. That's the 'subversive' work we do here.

"One of the greatest things we can do at SFBS, I think, is to educate the wealthy and privileged in our society about their wealth and privilege. It's an unofficial, unspoken policy of the Food Bank, but I think it's important to remind the privileged that poor people exist. Anyone working in the food line can't forget, because they're faced with it every day. They're faced with the fact that the poor are young, old, black, white, they have kids, they are kids – and recognizing that is really important.

"Tutors here go another step. They talk to the poor and see why, so often, their situation is not of their choosing. And how complex their problems often are. We deal with a perception from the outside that we should be able to get these people in here, teach them to read and spit them out employable. But the reality is, we're so far from being able to do that.

"I had a young businessman come in here, for example, scoping us out to see if he wanted to donate. He demanded that I give him two success stories. I started telling him about Meng."

Meng, 43, came from the Mien hill tribe in

Laos. In 1975, when the U.S. military pulled out of its "secret war" in that country, Meng's farming village of 60 people had to flee the oncoming communist Pathet Lao. Meng had not been a soldier in the guerrilla war against the Pathet Lao, but one of his relatives had, which put his life in danger. His village was napalmed, and everyone in it faced execution if caught. Carrying their two children in their arms and all their belongings on their backs, Meng and his wife walked nearly a month through jungle and mountain terrain, finally reaching the Mekong River and escaping into Thailand. Coming from a primitive, rural culture with no written language, Meng had no idea of where to go, other than the squalid refugee camp offered by the Thai government. The family, which grew with two more children, lived in one room and was permitted to leave the camp only by special permission on one-day passes. But the city outside was terrifying and unwelcoming, and moving across the world to unknown countries seemed unthinkable. They lived in the camp ten years, until Thailand decided it would no longer support the refugees. Meng's family was given a choice: move to Canada, Australia or the U.S., or return to Laos and face death.

Meng decided to join a distant cousin in a place called Sacramento, California. He got help tracking the cousin down and asking him to sponsor his family. Having never read nor written anything in any language, the family was given a six-month's "education" in the English alphabet and American customs before being put on a plane to San Francisco.

Now, nearly ten years later and with five children, Meng is one of the Reading Center's most avid students. He has learned to read and write competently. His English, although heavily accented, is nearly fluent. He has learned to drive a car, and he spends much of his time shuttling his children back and forth from school and appointments. His two oldest sons are straight 'A' students in high school, and help their father on his assignments.

As Usher was telling the story of Meng's success to the businessman, Usher recalls, "He cut me off in the middle and said, 'Yeah, but does he have a job?'

"The fact is, Meng is overwhelmed by even walking into a copy shop. Although he has worked as a part-time pizza delivery driver, he can't conceive that he is capable of having a job beyond that. He doesn't believe his English is good enough. And in Sacramento, even though we have the largest Mien population in the U.S., there is no entry-level employment for the Mien, as there are restaurants for Chinese, gardening businesses for Latinos."

Meng, from a culture where 40 is well past middle-age, sees his job as preparing his children for successful lives as U.S. citizens. In that, he has triumphed.

The young woman in the wheelchair is another example, says Usher, of a success story using measurements other than the workplace. "She comes in every day, and uses our typing tutor on the computer. She started typing two words a minute, and now types about 25-28. We heard of a job requiring someone to type just 20 words a minute. She went to the job interview, and they *wanted* to give her the job, but when she got there, she froze and could type only a word a minute. She can't function in a stress environment. It's just fear. She'll get there eventually, but she's not going to get there in two months."

On Usher's wall is a picture drawn by six-year-old Timothy, one of several neighborhood latchkey children who seek refuge in the Reading Center while waiting for a school bus, or hang out there after school when nobody is home. Timothy, who like most six-year-old boys loves cars and trucks, has drawn a picture of a police car. There are stars on each car door, and lights on the roof. A white policeman is in

the driver's seat, a large gun protruding from his window. In the back, behind a screen, is a black man, in custody. Overhead, a helicopter shines lights and points guns down at the car.

"That's Timothy's future, as he sees it," says Usher, pointing to the man in the back of the car. "His cousin, who is 18, just got out of prison. Dad is nowhere to be found, and mom is half-functioning. Can you imagine being six years old and having a mother who never really wakes up, walking past prostitutes who are the same color as you are, who are the role models for your nine-year-old sister?"

Usher keeps the drawing on his wall as a reminder, for those days when clients fail to show up, or drop out or haven't done their homework.

"We get them after the damage has been done," he says. "You don't just turn around 25 years of abuse, of having your self-esteem torn from you every day, in just three hours a week. You don't. But it's tremendously important to try."

AUDREY

THE 1950S IN RURAL LOUISIANA WERE A TIME and place where children didn't often question their parents' decisions, and parents didn't often discuss their reasoning. And when young Audrey Blackmon, now 45, was told she'd have to stay home, clean house and babysit younger siblings rather than go to school like all the other kids in the neighborhood, she had little choice but to agree.

"My mom just didn't think I needed education," she recalls. "And, you know, whatever the parents said, that's what went. I really wanted to go to school. It's just that my mom wasn't the type of person you could sit down and try to tell her what direction to go."

Audrey speaks in a soft, melodious Lousiana dialect. She sits on a green sofa in her immaculate South Sacramento apartment, where a photograph of her oldest son getting his high school diploma is as prominently displayed as a painting of the Last Supper. Occasionally, she shakes her head slowly, as if amazed at her own story.

"I wanted to marry, so I could get out of the house," Audrey said. Because she was "nothin' but a kid," the only way conceivable for her to leave home and survive was by getting pregnant and being "forced" to get married, she explains.

"That's the way it was. I know it wasn't the right way to go, but when you want out...." she pauses and takes a breath. "So, I was 14 when I got pregnant and got out.

"But still I didn't go to school. Once you start having kids, you know, things change. You'll be out there nothin' but a child yourself, and you'll be under the impression, 'Well, I can make it.' But as you get older, and learn the real world, you realize you're not really making it. You're only surviving."

Audrey survived on welfare, raising five children by the time she was 27. Her marriage to the father of her first three children, a man with a 9th grade education, lasted six years. With not a day of schooling, she could barely print her name.

"It was a gift from God I could even catch a bus," she recalls. "I was afraid to ask people directions because you never know which way they're going to send you.

"It was a darkness on the inside," she recalls. "You carry a fear, because there's so much out there you can't deal with. If you even think on the order of a job, you think education. You think, 'I can't do that. I can't read, I can't write. I can't even hold a good strong conversation because I wonder what people are talking about.' I mean, when you're not educated, you're limited to a certain amount of things, certain conversations, certain places you can go and fit in. It's a fear you carry with you everywhere."

Audrey was determined her children would go to school. "It was just always in my heart," she says. "I didn't want them to be like me. I just felt like there was more and I didn't want them to live in darkness. I couldn't describe what I was missing, but I know I didn't want them in the darkness I felt."

When her children would come home from school, she'd secretly look at their homework. "I'd wonder, 'How do they learn it? How does it stay in your brain?'"

When Audrey's 16-year-old daughter, Lynelle, dropped out of high school in Baton Rouge, Audrey took her to a continuation school in hopes she'd stick it through to a diploma.

"When I went there that day to sign her up, I had no idea that was my day. But just out of the blue I asked the man, 'Do y'all take older people here too?' and he said, 'Yeah, you never get too old to learn.'" Terrified but excited, Audrey began her education. She was 39.

"I'll never forget," she says of the first difficult days of school. "I always could count in my head, but I couldn't do figures on paper. A lady there would explain it to me, but then she would walk away. I used to absolutely get a headache trying to figure it out, but I would give myself pep talks." She whispers, as she whispered to herself in those days: "One day, I'm gonna have a breakthrough!"

"I would ask them to give me a couple of problems, so I could practice those little problems over and over and over. I would come home, lay across the bed, and I'd work: add, subtract, add.

"I remember sometimes it got so hard, I used to wake up in the morningtime and tell myself, 'If I only learn but one thing. One word, or one whatever. Just one thing.'

"My kids weren't too much help, because they didn't have the patience I needed. And when you're anxious to learn, and then a person is treating you like you should already know these things, this put a damper on me. I got so I didn't want to ask anyone, because I didn't want anybody to confuse me. And I didn't want them to make me think I should know it already. So I asked the teachers to put a few little problems and words on paper. I would study them 'till I thought I was going blind. And I'd always tell myself, the harder that it got, 'I'm gonna have a breakthrough.' And I would. Little by little. Word by word.

"I can truly say, by the grace of God, I did it, on my own."

When Audrey and two of her children moved to Sacramento in 1993, she could read simple words and do simple computations. The welfare department directed her to an adult school, where she found large classes that moved too quickly and offered no individual attention.

"I saw myself not learning anything, so I just left. I got the telephone and I started calling and calling. I was determined to find somewhere to go to school, and finally I came across Craig (Usher). He's sweet, and he's got more patience!"

Audrey's tutor is Don Day, retired from teaching Latin at a suburban high school, who volunteers at the Reading Center twice a week with his wife, Carolina.

Don says he is re-learning the rules of English grammar in the process of tutoring Audrey, and has also learned something about determination.

"She's so motivated, it's a pleasure," Don says. Watching her learn to read as an adult, he says, has caused him to "really believe it is a miracle that we learn how to read. How you can start tying words together and seeing them. It's amazing, really."

In nearly two years of work with Don, Audrey has progressed from struggling with simple words to being able to read newspapers, menus, signs and instructions.

"Sometimes I have her read a story. She's written me a letter, and did a nice job on that. She's really doing quite well. She doesn't need a lot of help, she just needs someone to stick with her."

Don and Audrey consider themselves friends, although their relationship is confined to the learning process that takes place in the tiny,

windowless Reading Center room. Don and Carolina's three-bedroom house, like Audrey's apartment, is spotless and decorated with religious artifacts and family photographs. But the Days' home is in a middle-class, mostly white suburb, and Blackmon's apartment is in a predominantly black, South Sacramento neighborhood. Both Don and Audrey acknowledge that were it not for the Reading Center, they would not likely have a conversation with each other, let alone a relationship. And Don concedes that, prior to his tutoring experience, he might have had a "more negative impression" – hardly the overwhelming admiration he now feels – if someone had described to him Audrey, a completely uneducated African-American woman who had lived most of her

life on welfare.

From SFBS' point of view, the success story here is not just Audrey's education, but Don's.

Audrey says her work with Don is "not easy, but it's comfortable. "I feel good with my surroundings, because I'm able to ask questions any time there's things I don't understand. And I think I've progressed more than before, because I don't have the fear. I still have some trouble with my big words – sometimes I still got a fright there. But I read! And I'm getting better."

The greatest blessing to come from her education, Audrey says, is the ability to shake her lifelong dependency on welfare.

"After you've been on that welfare for years, it becomes a way of life, you know? You've got to report to them how much money is yours, if you get a raise. I thank God for all the years of help, but I'm so grateful it's over. Work makes you independent, because you're counting on what *you* work for, not what they're gonna give you. You're not worried if they're going to cut you off, you don't have to fill out no paper once a year to explain everything. It's a better way of life."

Now Audrey works nights at a convalescent home. She has overcome the fear of buying groceries without food stamps, and feels confident budgeting paychecks, instead of welfare checks. "I would have never gone for a job if I couldn't read," she says. "I was always too scared, because I knew there would always be some reading involved." For example, she says, "What if you do motel work, and there's a note in the room for you 'not to do this', or to 'do this'? And if you couldn't read it, you'd lose the job.

"When you look back and see where you came from, that gives you motivation to go on, you know? I don't walk in the fear that I used to walk in. I feel more comfortable when I go to the grocery store, when I do any shopping. Studying for my driver's license, I feel good. I can pick up the newspaper, I can pick up a menu. I can read my Bible.

"I just can't put it into words, but it's a whole different world. All the things that I couldn't imagine myself doing, I want to do. I want to travel. I'm not fearful any more of going to a bus. I can pick up the bus schedule and find the right one. I love the news, and I understand what they're saying now. I love to be able to read signs. It used to be, I'd pick up a menu, and everything was in total darkness."

Audrey has begun to realize, she says, that there will always be new challenges that seem frightening.

"Sometimes, like on the job, if they're checking in a new client I almost shake, because there's so much to know. Then, once you get into it, you do it. And you see there wasn't that much to fear."

"I know one thing," she concludes. "Whatever you start doing to change yourself, if you decide 'no matter how hard it gets, I'm gonna keep on,' you'll get there. Because the more you learn, the more you're not going to want to stop."

Havens resident Glynda Schaeffer with her children, Haley Kay and Tyler James

HOUSING THE HOMELESS

HAVENS TRANSITIONAL HOUSING

MARCH 1988

Dear Friends,

The urgent phone call came during an evening meeting on Food Bank business. The caller told me he was at a motel on Stockton Boulevard, a seedy section of the city. He and his wife had taken in a young woman and three small children who were evicted by the motel manager. The woman was pregnant, no place to go, and could I help?

I was about to explain that I run only food programs and have nothing to do with housing. Then it struck me I had better practice what I preach. I heard myself say, "Give me your address and room number. I'll be down to see you in an hour."

Charles Sylva went with me.

We found a raunchy motel of the cheapest kind. In the dim lighting we saw the number we were looking for and a black man opened the door to our knock. His wife smiled at us in greeting and a small, obviously pregnant young woman stared at us without expression from a thin, pale face. Three toddlers, aged three, two and one, lay on the bed. They each wore a diaper and nothing else.

The mother may have been 20, but her speech and manner indicated extreme immaturity and little education. She and her husband had driven from Arkansas earlier in the week. We could imagine the rest. No job. No money. Three babies needing everything only money could buy. Did the man decide the wife could do better without him? Whatever he thought, he had left her high and dry, totally adrift.

Charles and I talked to the motel manager. He was an Asian, living with his wife and teenaged son in rooms as dingy as the rest of the motel. He didn't want the young woman in his motel. For one thing, her room had been a mess to clean up that morning. And then there was the matter of payment. He assured us he was not unfeeling. But too many times he'd been tricked by promises to pay later. When I told him I was a priest, he relented and said she could stay one more night. He charged me $33 for one room, one night.

Charles and I saw the room - a cramped, small space with a stained, worn covering on the bed. I would have sat up all night rather than lie on that bed.

Before we left, I assured the weary, beaten-down young mother that we would send her help in the morning. The black couple helped her move the three barefoot children to the other room. She carried all her worldly goods in three grocery bags.

We drove back to the rectory in a kind of numb speechlessness. We were asking ourselves what is wrong with a society that produces such a family as this. What happened along the way? Who brought this woman into the world and allowed her to receive so little education? How did things get so hopeless and bogged down?

Neither of us had answers. I could only think of Our Lord's words. He said we are welcome into His kingdom if we clothe the naked and feed the hungry and shelter the homeless and comfort the afflicted.

If we don't do these things, we are not welcome.

May God bless you all,

Fr. Dan Madigan

My Dear Food Bank Friends:

The food locker windows have shown me poverty, and the soup kitchen tables have certainly added their share. But it is the nighttime rectory door knocks that have exposed me to the fear and stress of the homeless family. The late evenings of the 1960's in Del Paso Heights often brought families to our door. They came for a religious blessing. They came for some consolation. They came because one of them was leaving the next morning for Viet Nam.

Night-time still brings weather-beaten families to our rectory door here in Oak Park. They come now because of today's war – the war of having nowhere to lay their heads.

These unwanted and isolated parents are afraid to take their children to the homeless shelter. The angry outbursts, explosive behaviors and cultural clashes that they know or think exist there frightens them. They willingly accept sleeping mats on our open porch. They are even pleased to bed down in the newspaper collection truck as it offers them the privacy, safety and quietness they long for so much.

Derelicts, drifters and hobos are not the only homeless people in California. Half of the Golden State's 2.3 million hungry are children and so are one-third of its 150,000 homeless.

Having no home disintegrates a family. It wears away morale and self-esteem. It has disastrous effects on physical health. The hardship of having to rough it in conditions of poor nutrition and squalor takes its toll. Children begin to exhibit aggressive behavior, hyperactivity and signs of depression. Adults come up with diseases such as chronic bronchitis, emphysema and tuberculosis.

My friends, as God-loving people we cannot stand by and ignore this situation. It's not right we do so. We have to help put together an atmosphere of warmth, affection and affirmation for these wounded families. Please join me.

With every good wish,

Fr. Dan Madigan

Dear Friends:

Three days after Thanksgiving - Sunday, November 26 - I left the tranquility of my new home in Clarksburg and drove to the Oak Park Soup Kitchen which is housed at Immaculate Conception Church. This 13-minute journey plunged me back into my pre-September world in which I had lived for 13 years. Now things seemed altogether different to me. My ten weeks away from this scene had brought about great change — all of which I discovered was within myself.

I was flabbergasted by the long line of ragged people. Their hungry faces, weather-beaten appearances, missing teeth and unkempt children seemed all so new to me. Had I forgotten that fast? Had I become a victim of my often stated claim, "out of sight is truly out of mind"?

A 40-ish man clad in summer attire asked for a private word with me. He was cold and wanted a warm jacket — nothing more. I told him to wait and I would be back in ten minutes with help. When I returned later he was gone. Mario, Al, Lee and Art were locking up the building. They could not understand why the door to the men's toilet was locked and why their keys would not open it.

As we were all about to leave, I noticed the toilet door move ever so slightly. Someone was in there. I called out, identified myself and said I was sending for the police unless the occupant came out. He did. It was the gentleman who had requested the jacket. He did not believe I would return. He had no home. He had no clothes. He had found himself a 3 x 5-foot concrete toilet floor for the night. He intended to stay there. He was secure.

Moments later, a husband and wife with three tiny children drove up. A battered automobile was their home and had been for some time. They needed anything we could offer — a hot meal, food, blankets, lodging, gasoline money, clothing. Above all they needed a kind face and an understanding heart. We fitted that bill. They now live in one of our houses. The father is working and their Christmas will be warm.

Friends, as we celebrate this Christmas let's remember that there are many Josephs, lots of Marys and several Jesuses looking for food and lodging on our streets. The fact that we don't see them in our immediate neighborhood does not mean they don't exist. They do.

With every good wish,

Fr. Dan Madigan

Homes, not Shelters

LIVING THERE ON 32ND AND BROADWAY, in the rectory of Immaculate Conception Church, people came to the door any time of day and into the night. At 10:00 or 11:00 at night, they'd ring the bell, begging for a place to spend the night. Sometimes, over their shoulder, you'd see their battered old automobile, and the little faces of their children peering out of the window. Little kids. You'd have to be a man of iron to say "no".

Still, there wasn't much you could do. There was no point in sending them to the Salvation Army, because it was too late at night, and it was also too late for the shelters. I rarely had enough money to give them for a night's stay in a motel.

I could have brought them into the house, and put them down in the basement. But the house was attached to the church, and both the house and the church were all wooden. I was scared to death if I ever brought them in we'd have a fire from a lighted cigarette.

So I'd offer them cushions on the veranda outside the door. They were absolutely delighted. They only wanted to be assured they'd be safe.

I would say, "I am going to bed, and there will be nobody coming out of this door for the rest of the night. If the police drive by here they can't very well see you, but should they give you any kind of a hassle, just ring the doorbell and I will be right down to take care of it."

Once they got that type of security they loved it.

The other favorite place for housing people was a big trailer we used to store newspapers for recycling. Families would feel very secure in there. These people had tremendous fears. Many were afraid to go to the shelters. The shelters would separate them, men from women, and I got the impression they were really noisy places.

In 1980, I cut off a section of the rectory I lived in, and built an apartment in there. A lot of people were staying for the night only, but we had a goodly number of people there over the years.

Five years later, a woman named Jessie Mays died, and left me her house. She wasn't Catholic, and I didn't know anything about her until she died and gave me the house. She had come to church on an Easter Sunday and left a donation. I had written her a thank-you note, and apparently it moved her, because she'd left the note in a prominent spot in her home. I guess that's why she gave me the house on 38th Street. I sold the house to Bishop Quinn to raise money for our Food Bank programs. Shortly after that, I turned around and asked him to give me the house back, to use for a homeless program. He did, and we named the house after him.

Behind that house, we built a little cottage out of a garage. The gentleman that helped me build it was (former state Assemblyman, now Judge) Lloyd Connelly. I think I went through more in the way of permits and problems to get the little garage converted into a house than if I was building a high-rise.

I suppose I was into housing people almost as long as I was into the food program. I didn't think of it as a housing program at the time, but when I look back on it, I realize it was.

Seeing these small homes being put to good use, we put the Havens Transitional Housing Board together in 1990. I knew that if you got an idea of putting a building together for the homeless, say, an apartment complex, you'd have to go through a tremendous amount of hassle. You'd have to sell it to the neighborhood, and sell it to the city, and get permits of all kinds. But I found out that if you have a home, you can house up to six adults who are not related to each other, without any permit.

Since then, generous people have donated four houses, two duplexes and a fourplex. In 1994 alone, Havens provided housing and mentoring for 21 families, a group of nine farm workers, and 68 individuals.

I still think this idea of donated homes scattered throughout the neighborhoods is a great system. Because if you throw a whole bunch of homeless people in with each other, what do they see? They see each other. Whereas if you put somebody into a neighborhood, they see people getting up in the morning and going to work, taking their kids to school, mowing the lawn and keeping things clean. And they are away from the stigma of homelessness. Even though our houses are fairly close together, they don't carry any badge of "homelessness" about them. Sensitive to the "homeless" label, our board changed the program's original name, from Homeless Havens to Havens Transitional Housing.

It seems to me that anywhere there is homelessness, if churches or non-profits pulled together and bought abandoned or dilapidated homes, fixed them up and "adopted them" for homeless families, this could mushroom into a huge and wonderful program. Most churches can afford to put a down payment on an inexpensive home, and just make payments on it like anyone else. Buy it, then get the community behind it.

AKENNYA'S HOUSE

"HOLD STILL," AKENNYA ADMONISHES HER 7-year-old daughter, Lakeisha. The girl sits cross-legged on the floor, back to her mother, thin arms wedged between her mother's knees as Akennya carefully brushes her hair, twisting it into ponytails finished off with colorful barrettes.

"No, you're not wearing those gym shoes," Akennya repeats to eldest daughter LaKenya, 8. "I told you, the laces are too dirty. We need bleach. Wear your sandals today."

Louis, 5, and Latoya, 3, have already been taken to day care on the bus this early summer morning. Now Akennya prepares for another bus ride to the Oak Park Community Center, where her two oldest girls take classes in karate and crafts.

Raising four young children, going to college and keeping a two-bedroom house spotless would be a challenge for most mothers. Many wouldn't bother with details like bleaching the kids' shoelaces, even if they had the daily help and support of a husband and father, and a car for ferrying the children back and forth to classes.

But 26-year-old Akennya, single and once homeless, has had so many obstacles to overcome in life, so little control over difficult circumstances, she's sometimes extra vigilant about details under her control. Her children are well-mannered and affectionate. Akennya is adamant that they'll grow up with love and positive role models.

"My mom worked two jobs and wasn't hardly around us when we were little," Akennya recalls. Her father was a drug dealer who slapped and verbally abused her mother when he was around. When Akennya was about five, her mother fled the abuse, moving the children from Detroit to Chicago. Akennya's mother struggled to support her family but was rarely at home.

"When we were teenagers, we just went out in the streets to get whatever we didn't get at home," Akennya recalls.

Akennya started smoking marijuana at age 12, and dropped out of school in the 11th grade when she became pregnant with her first child. Akennya's drug-dealing father had reappeared in her life, long enough to introduce his daughter to crack cocaine. She became addicted after the birth of her first daughter, LaKenya.

For seven years, Akennya lived off and on with her children's father in his parents' home, scrounging for drugs and leaving when he became abusive. She "hit bottom" after social workers threatened to take her children away if she didn't stick with a drug recovery program.

"Even then I wasn't ready to stop," Akennya recalls. She left a drug program after a month, went to the other side of town and moved in with drug-abusing relatives. Having spent her welfare check and sold their refrigerator for drugs, Akennya realized she faced eviction, homelessness and the loss of her children.

Even getting high couldn't hide the fact that she was neglecting her own children, and Akennya was miserable. She called her caseworker for help and began the tortuous work of freeing herself from addiction.

After two years of staying off drugs, Akennya had her GED and a job as a co-counselor at Haymarket House, the Chicago drug treatment program that helped her through recovery. It was time to rid herself of another bad habit — the abusive relationship with the father of her children.

Akennya and the children left Chicago for Houston, where her brother was living. Her brother had promised good job opportunities and a place to stay, but by the time Akennya and the kids arrived, he'd left for California. Akennya wound up in a homeless shelter where she was separated from her children.

"We cried every day. It was so bad," she recalls. Finally she reached her brother in Sacramento, and loaded up her '81 Ford Escort to head to California. An hour out of Houston, the car broke down. After hours of trying to flag down help, a couple stopped

and helped Akennya's family of five pile all their belongings, bundled in garbage bags and boxes, onto a Greyhound bus.

It wasn't until two years later, when Akennya was settled in a two-bedroom home in the Havens program, that she wrote the check for the final payment on that car left in Shulenberg, Texas.

Akennya and her children were referred to Sacramento Food Bank Services' transitional housing program by a city-sponsored homeless shelter. SFBS' Havens program accepts residents who are willing to sign a contract with the program, agreeing to work with mentors on a specific plan to gain the skills necessary to avoid a return to homelessness.

The program requires participants to keep a budget, balance their checkbooks, pay off debts, meet regularly with mentors, keep their homes clean and attend counseling where needed. At the end of three months, residents must either be working or attending school. Residents also set goals for themselves, ranging from paying off bills to attending college. For many, it is the first time anyone has helped them with basic skills like housekeeping and money management.

"The rent is 15 percent of your income, and they help you with your budget," Akennya explains. "The reason a lot of people become homeless is they can't manage their money. The way they've got it set

up, where you're allotted so much in the month to spend on phone bills, and food, the gas company – it's good. It's smart. It's a good thing to keep doing."

Budgeting didn't come easy for Akennya, who had never had a bank account or anyone to explain to her how to write a check. She began dutifully keeping receipts and writing down all purchases according to categories arranged with her mentor, Havens Program Director Paula Lamb. Groceries were entered in one column, transportation costs in another, and separate categories were filled out for payment of each monthly bill. Akennya met weekly with her mentor, and invariably discovered that a receipt or two had been lost in the jumble of her handbag, or that she'd confused her checkbook register with the program's monthly budget form. Instead of writing the name of the grocery store when she entered a check in the register, for example, she'd write "groceries," or "housekeeping supplies." Akennya is bright, but it has taken her months to overcome a frustration and sense of hopelessness that comes with a checkbook that never seems to balance.

"They don't expect you to be perfect, but at least to be trying," Akennya says. "They're not asking too much. I mean, just keeping up with your money, and they're helping you. Not everybody can take it – having to follow the rules, having to keep track of every dime – but if they really want to benefit from it, they will."

School has been even more successful. Akennya is enrolled at Sacramento City College, where she has earned 30 units and plans to continue studying to become a probation officer.

"She's really learned her way through the system," says mentor Paula. "She's applied for books ahead of time, and even got a grant of $500. She wanted to spend the money on new clothes for her kids, but I convinced her to save it for school expenses.

"Akennya's downfall when it comes to money is wanting her kids to have new clothes, new hair ornaments, three pairs of shoes each. It's hard for her to go to the Clothes Closet when she'd love to go to the mall."

Akennya also had to learn ways to discipline her children without using physical violence. Raised in an abusive environment and having suffered years with a man who beat her, Akennya's natural reaction to frustration with her children was to pull out a whipping belt. After parenting classes and counseling sessions, she now uses "time out" instead.

The family goes to church two evenings a week and every Sunday. Akennya, viewing her fundamentalist church as her salvation, tithes 10 percent of her meager income to the church. Church members help her mow her lawn, arranged a trip to Disneyland for Akennya and her kids, and provide constant support to the family.

Akennya looks forward to the day when she has a job, her own house in a nice neighborhood and a husband who will set a good example for her children, "just like the families you see on TV."

"I didn't have anyone to look up to when I was growing up," she says, "I did what I saw everybody else around me doing. And when I was using drugs, I didn't think about anything or anybody else."

Now she is determined to stay off the path taken by so many friends from childhood. Most are on drugs and welfare, their fatherless children born addicted to crack.

When Akennya's oldest daughter came home one day saying she admired the looks of one of the street walkers that frequent the neighborhood, Akennya and members of a newly formed Havens Residents' Council became involved with an anti-hooker patrol. When they spot "Johns" making deals with prostitutes, residents jot down the Johns' license plates, and inform police. Police then send warning letters to the home addresses of the men — a tactic that seems to have had a beneficial effect on the neighborhood.

"You've got to have positive role models around you," says Akennya. "And that's why I'm trying to be different for my kids."

THE STEPHENS FAMILY

DANNY STEPHENS KNEW HE HAD TO GET HIS homeless family off the riverbank the night he was fishing with his sons and bullets whistled by their heads. After nearly five months of sleeping outdoors in their truck, and in a series of cheap motels, the family of six was given temporary housing through the City of Sacramento, then referred to the Havens Transitional Housing program.

There, for the first time since their marriage as 20-year-olds 17 years ago, the parents of four teenaged boys learned how to manage their money, live within their limited means and plan for the future.

The family moved to Sacramento in 1991 from San Francisco, where they had paid reduced rent in a home owned by LaRae Stephens' grandmother. Conscientious parents, they didn't like raising their boys in the rough Mission District, where gangs and crime are rampant. And the price of Bay Area living was impossible to meet. Neither Danny nor LaRae had finished high school, and Danny's difficulty with reading limited him to manual labor.

Once in Sacramento, LaRae drove a school bus, Danny worked in a wrecking yard, and the family remained close and loving, despite financial pressures. When Danny hurt his back and lost his job, however, the couple found no safety net large enough to spare them from homelessness.

"We were doing okay for awhile," says LaRae. "But we were paying $650 a month rent for a house, and I was only bringing home about $800 a month. With four kids, we just got deeper and deeper into debt. The only way we could figure out to get out of debt was to move out of the place we were in, and move in with my sister for awhile."

Relatives were only willing to house the large family for short periods of time, and their debts kept them from renting even a cramped, inexpensive apartment. So, on many bitter cold nights from January through April, the family slept on the banks of the Sacramento River. They chose a spot 12 miles downriver from urban Sacramento, near the tiny Delta community of Freeport.

"We didn't know at the time, but it was just across the river and down a bit from Father Dan's church in Clarksburg," says LaRae. "I'm sure he would've helped us then if we'd known to talk to him."

Danny and Brian, 17, and David, 15, slept outdoors on the riverbank, on a level stretch of dirt between the river and the steep bank of the levee. Their spot was sheltered by oaks and clear of thorny brush. To avoid being rousted from the spot by police, who arrested people for camping, they brought along fishing gear. When a car approached, they'd jump up from their sleeping bags, and cast a line.

LaRae and the two youngest boys, Christopher, 14, and William, 12, slept in the family's covered pickup truck on the levee road above the campsite. Every few nights, after LaRae got paid, the family would rent a cheap motel room in order to shower and sleep in a warm room.

"The kids were in school, I continued going to work and Danny had started training with Goodwill, in janitorial," recalls LaRae, in an interview with the family in their new living room. "We were trying to keep everything basically as normal as possible – a structure – but every night we didn't know what we were going to do, depending how much I made that week."

Nobody at LaRae's company was aware the family was homeless. She was too proud to let the family's situation be known.

Danny, who has been less vocal than outgoing LaRae, finally looks up and meets his interviewer's eyes. Like the tattoo of Casper the Ghost on his forearm, Danny reveals both toughness and a gentle innocence. The couple's sons, lanky adolescents, gather around their parents and listen quietly, respectfully, to stories of their family's ordeals.

"One night, Chris, Brian and David and I were down on the riverbank fishing," Danny recalls. "The kids were starting to go to sleep, and all of a sudden this guy starts coming over and shooting his gun at us. Two shots – one in the water and one whistling right by us.

"I won't ever forget that sound."

The family was desperate for housing, and was accepted for temporary homeless quarters through the city of Sacramento before being offered a two-bedroom home, around the corner from Akennya's house, through SFBS' Havens program. For the next two years, they were coached in money management skills, helped to pay off their debts and taught how to save by buying groceries in bulk and avoiding impulse purchases. Danny acknowledged his drinking had contributed to the couple's problems, quit using alcohol, and the couple went to parenting classes to help them deal with four adolescent boys.

"It was hard at first, because I felt like they were invading our privacy," Danny says. "Then we realized, hey, we're down here, and we want to move up. If they can show us how to do it, we'll stick with it."

Havens Program Director Paula Lamb says motivation is the primary quality she looks for in potential clients. "Motivation to make changes in their lives," Lamb says. "We're looking for honesty, not denial. People who are willing to face up to their debts or substance abuse problems, and move on to meet new goals." It wasn't easy for the Stephenses or Akennya to stick with the program, but both families were motivated.

"They were always there whenever we needed advice or just to talk with someone," says LaRae. "When we ran low on food, Lori, who runs the Food Locker, would say, 'Come on over, honey, we'll help you.' We made some wonderful friends there."

Most importantly, the family was given the breathing space and shown the skills needed to put them back on their feet. They cut $200 off their monthly grocery bill by such simple measures as buying hamburger in inexpensive three-pound bulk packages, and breaking them down into smaller portions for the freezer. They buy generic groceries instead of name brands, and buy vegetables at the farmers' market. They've cut their smoking habit by half,

working towards quitting altogether. LaRae, who's always enjoyed shopping after work with friends, still shops but doesn't buy anything she doesn't really need.

"We were looking at going from a shelter straight to an apartment, and really not learning anything, before we found out about Havens Transitional Housing," says LaRae. "We would have wound up right back where we were. But the program showed us where we made our mistakes, how to correct them, and how not to make them again."

In the summer of 1995, after two years in the Havens program, the Stephenses moved into a rental duplex they found through a program that provides low-rent housing for families who help rehabilitate abandoned homes in distressed neighborhoods.

On a summer evening, one week after moving into the freshly painted home near Sacramento's Southside Park, Danny and LaRae reflect on their goals.

One day, says LaRae, they'll get high school diplomas and save up enough to qualify for a housing program that will help them build their own home. Meanwhile, Danny looks forward to giving something back. He returns to SFBS to help fix up Havens houses. This year, for the first time, the couple hopes to donate toys for other homeless families at Christmas, through the program that filled their children's wish lists in the past.

"I'll definitely donate," says Danny, suddenly animated. "Somebody donated for us, and I'm grateful for what they did."

Luz Maria Torres and son Ambrosio

NURTURING OUR CHILDREN

MOTHER-BABY PROGRAM

OCTOBER 1992

Dear Friends:

I am sure you will agree that a family of four cannot live on a yearly income of $12,700. Yet one in every five children in our country are surviving – if not living – in such a household.

Daily we work with such families. They are where our food outlets are. In Oak Park, Del Paso Heights, Rancho Cordova and North Sacramento.

The families we see are truly hungry. They are really hurting. Their children are in need of immediate help.

That's why we have designed a new program. Our Mother-Baby Program will make a difference. It will help salvage many of Sacramento's impoverished infants.

Don't let the magnitude of what we are up against keep you from stepping forward to help. Join us, please. The children we see need you.

As always, my kindest regards and best wishes to you.

Fr. Dan Madigan

Dear Friends:

There seems to be strong public opinion today that California is taking a nosedive. That crime, gangs, narcotics, poverty and homelessness are on the increase. And strong family life is quickly deteriorating.

The United Nations is proclaiming this year of 1994 as "The Year of the Family." It seems all countries are craving for the return of the strong parenting days of old.

We here at SFBS feed, clothe, house and educate people. We run baby programs and senior programs. But by far the most important thing we do is bridge building — forming linkages, alliances and mentoring relationships between people who have and people who don't.

As far as I can see, mentoring is the only true answer.

Osmosis works and works well. Whether a person is among the "haves" or "have nots" has everything to do with the possession of, or lack of, good rearing, healthy discipline and proper values. The designation as a "have" or "have not" has much, much less to do with mere material possessions.

If you agree with my thinking, please join us. We will give you the opportunity for the daily dispensing of services. And, above all, we will give you the opportunity of imparting to people our philosophy of self-empowerment.

With every best wish to you and yours,

Fr. Dan Madigan

MAY 1995

Dear Friends:

When hungry and destitute people come to our door we greet them with "hand out" hospitality. Before they leave we gently tell them of our "hand up" programs. Some return. And through involvement with us many do get back on their feet.

The recipe for escaping poverty is simple. Finish high school. Get a job. Stay in the labor market. Get married as an adult. Stay married.

The media constantly outlines our country's ills. Crime, drugs, poverty, illiteracy, homelessness, etc. But seldom does it mention what may well be our biggest and most basic problem. Illegitimacy.

A recent study found that children born to females who finished high school, got married and reached age 20 before having their first child, lived in poor households at a rate of 8%. By contrast children born to mothers who did none of these things had a poverty rate of 79%.

Catch-22 has become a common phrase. It means being boxed in, having no escape options, no solutions.

We here at SFBS work with Catch-22 people. And through your help and generosity we many times remove for them horrendous obstacles, entrapments and dilemmas.

Please continue to stay in touch with us. You are truly the backbone of our efforts. And, yes, together we are making a big difference for many people.

With every good wish,

Fr. Dan Madigan

Dear Friends:

Every language possesses a large store of proverbs. The following ones pertain to the characteristics of parents and their offspring. "Apples don't fall far from the tree." "It is natural for the
fawn of a deer to have fleetness." "What would you expect from a cat but a kitten?" "Birds of
the same feather fly together."

Now, how about you? What was your upbringing like? Were you born a gosling, a chicken or
a turkey? Irish writer Alice Taylor explains the difference.

"The goose liked to make her own nest and line it inside with soft down. The gander for his
part was a most responsible father and guarded his goose on the nest; if you came too close he
flapped his wings and stretched out his long neck to bite you. The young goslings were fluffy
and yellow as butter and the goose and gander led them daily to the water where they all
washed and swam around happily. But the males in the turkey and hen families were irrespon-
sible fathers; once they had made their original contribution they disclaimed all responsibility
for the consequences.

"Great care had to be taken of the baby turkeys as they were a bit stupid and, unlike the
chickens and goslings, had a tendency to get lost. The goose was a very good mother and she
had a strong family unit working for her; the ordinary hen was the head of a one-parent family but her mothering instinct was fantastic. The turkey, on the other hand, had neither factor
going for her; she was on her own and she was not unduly concerned about the well-being of
her young. She needed a strong social welfare system to back her up and, of course, we provided that.

"Minding the turkeys was one of the chores of my young days. They had endless ways of going wrong. If they fell on their backs they could not right themselves; they could ramble off
through the long grass and, with no sense of direction, get totally lost, and their mother
would never bother to answer their plaintive 'peep-peep'."

So, good reader, if you had a great upbringing, truly thank God for it. In gratitude embrace
the helping and uplifting of less fortunate people.

With every good wish to you,

Fr. Dan Madigan

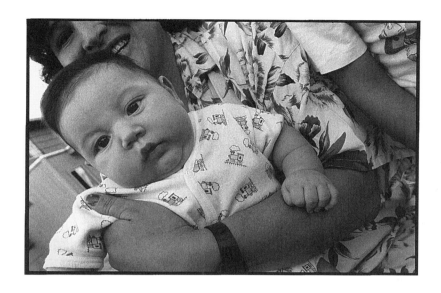

I WAS THE YOUNGEST IN MY FAMILY BY eight years, so I was never around babies growing up. Other than visits with my nephews and nieces, and the brief ritual of baptizing, I really had nothing to do with babies. So when I started the Food Bank, I was very conscious of the fact that babies had to be fed, and that's all. Any sensitivity I have toward babies I picked up from the volunteers. To my surprise, they started coming in to me saying, "You can't treat children the way we're treating them."

"What do you mean?" I asked. "The mom brings them in, says she has two, three, six or however many people in her family, babies or teenagers, and we give them food accordingly. What's wrong with that?"

The volunteers asked, "What about the little infants?" I didn't know what they ate. I was aware we had some kind of food for them, and had a very vague idea it was a formula – like milk.

But a number of volunteers were extremely upset that mothers with infants would say, "Give me whatever you have for the baby." They explained how you can't just give a baby milk-based formula one day, and soy-based the next, or try to give cereal to an infant. Many of the mothers in line didn't seem to know the difference any better than I did, and these experienced mothers who were volunteers worried after the babies' health. They also said the babies needed diapers.

That being the case, I suggested we'd better set up some sort of independent system, where the babies and toddlers wouldn't come to the window in the regular lines. We needed to do something more sensitive that would give these young moms a chance to talk to the volunteers.

To begin with, we thought we'd better find out the thinking of other people who work with mothers and babies. So we brought together a number of big players – health providers and people from the county's Health and Welfare Department and such, to see if we could get some help getting this off the ground.

It was a very disappointing meeting. The fellow from the health department started off saying that in his experience, any "grassroots" agency like ours that wanted to become multifaceted, as we were suggesting, usually went under. He said we should do what we knew how to do, and that's feed people. The feeling was that we'd be in over our heads.

At the same time, he informed me there was a program already in existence in Oak Park, providing formula, immunizations and such things to babies at a community center. I asked him how many people they saw a week, and the number he gave me was terribly small, something like 20 a week.

And he said to me, "How many kids would *you* expect?" I said, "I think we'd get about 80 a day."

"What in heavens name makes you think you would get 80 kids a day?" he asked. And I said that, well, from the lines we've had, I just kind of thought we would. All you needed was to open the door in the morning and 12 or 14 kids would fall right in on top of you.

I didn't see this assembled board going anywhere. The man from the county clearly wasn't supportive. The others were upbeat enough, but nobody offered any concrete plans. It looked as if the planning would go on forever and ever and ever, and that the program would never happen.

Maybe I was stronger in those days, or more stubborn. Because after this meeting I told myself, "I'm going to make this thing work, come hell or high water, I don't care what they say."

So, I got a number of moms together from among the volunteers. I asked them, "Okay,

if you have a baby, how many diapers does that baby use in a week?" I hadn't a clue. We figured a baby uses five diapers a day, on average. The cost of those diapers varies, depending on how big the baby is and where you buy the diapers.

But we came up with a cost of about 25 cents per diaper.

I figured we were looking at about 80 kids a day, and there were so many days in the year – gee, I thought, I'm $100,000 into this program before we even buy a drop of formula for these babies!

The big question was, where could we possibly get $100,000? Who's going to buy diapers? We looked around, and we found out that nobody wanted to buy diapers. The idea didn't seem to catch on. If anybody mentioned it to our donors, most of whom

are older, they would say, "Get them cloth diapers and let them wash them. I washed *my* diapers," and so forth. We'd have to explain that our clients don't have washers, don't have dryers, and some don't have homes. They don't have money to pay the electricity it costs to run those machines if they had them, or they don't have the soap, or the cars to go to the laundromat.

Right about that time a big article came out in the local newspaper, *The Sacramento Bee*, about diapers and the ecology. It rated cloth diapers and disposables on how much each type harmed the environment, and came up with a draw: if you use the cloth, you also must use water and soap, and gas or electricity to heat the water, but if you use the disposables you have the problem of waste disposal. At any rate, at least we could say we weren't advocating destroying the whole environment by promoting the use of disposable diapers.

Next I went to my friends, Senior Gleaners, Inc. asked them to help out, and they started giving us diapers. We bought some if we ran out of a size we needed, but primarily they donated them. Len McCandliss, president of Sierra Health Foundation, also had faith in our ability to get a program off the ground with the minimum of overhead, time-wasting and bureaucracy. He handed us a check for $25,000 to help the program get underway. And before we knew it, it worked! We had more than $100,000 worth of diapers. Today, we distribute close to 300,000 diapers a year.

We moved our administrative offices into the rear of the Food Bank warehouse and gave our old offices to the Mother-Baby program. We did a nice opening day, Bishop Quinn came, the TV cameras were there, we had baby food on the shelves and stacks and stacks of diapers.

At this opening day, which was somewhat chaotic with dozens of kids running about, food being served and cameras rolling, Executive Board member Bill Sparks and I were back in the diaper storage room. We hadn't gotten our system down precisely – just how to do all the packaging, and so forth. Bill was trying to put law and order into these stacks of diapers everywhere. People were running back, saying they wanted this or that size diaper.

We found there was the small/medium, the medium, the medium/large and in between, the boy and girl, the pull-on and something else. All these different boxes, 18 different sizes, and somebody would come in and say, "All I want is medium." And we'd stand there and say, "What do you mean by that?"

Here were these two men, he with some knowledge of diapers, I with absolutely none. We could be dealing with boxes of Kleenex, as far as I was concerned. In the middle of this conversation I said to Bill, "What in God's name is the difference between a boy diaper and a girl diaper?" And Bill said, "I'm sorry, we're too busy now for me to explain. One of these days you and I are going to go out for lunch, and I will sit down and explain the facts of life to you!"

Our grand opening was December 8, 1992, about the time we were having that year's holiday food drive. That year we started pushing for donations of baby food and formula. We didn't get too much formula, but we filled those shelves in there with baby food.

At the same time, formula companies had settled a lawsuit over unfair practices with an agreement to donate a certain amount of free formula to charities. In this area, Senior Gleaners, Inc. got elected to distribute the baby formula. Because the Gleaners are such good friends of ours, that settlement helped us a great deal.

Each year local chefs put on a fancy Food for Tots Dinner, with proceeds going to buy us more formula and baby food, and in three years that's brought in more than $65,000 for our Mother-Baby program. And, like so many of our activities, this one is like throwing seeds in the wind. It gets publicity, and raises the idea with people, and they contribute even if they don't attend. People are enormously generous.

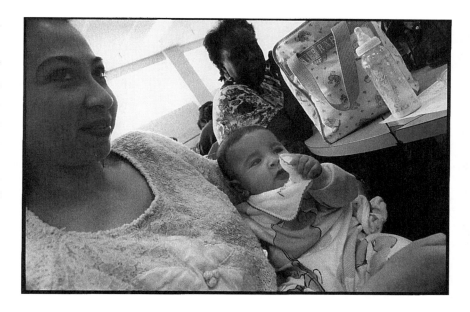

Without detracting from any of our other programs, I'd have to say the Mother-Baby program seems to have attracted the very best of volunteers. These are fantastic moms – people with tremendous sensibility and sensitivity, many of them with nursing backgrounds. Our idea is that when a mom – or sometimes a father or a grandparent – comes in, the volunteer takes them into a little room for awhile, gives them some very basic, common sense, down-to-earth, conversational-type counseling, then takes the mom out to give her diapers and food. Since we've started, we've also developed an educational program, where classes are offered twice a week in everything from parenting to budgeting and cooking nutritious, inexpensive meals.

When it became clear we needed to give these parents some education, we sat and thought, "How in heaven's name can we convince them to come in for classes?"

Well, Procter and Gamble has been very good to us, so we started offering some of the donations from Procter and Gamble as incentives for coming to class. Attend a class on cooking, and get a box of Tide, or Comet, or bars of soap. The classes were jammed, because they loved getting the laundry soap. To keep the size manageable, we eventually had to limit the giveaways to every fourth class each person attended. Soon, though, the women started coming not just for the soap, but because they enjoyed themselves there and learned some things. It's not just a class for these moms now, it's also a social event.

Our Mother-Baby classes and events have developed into a remarkable melting pot. Hill tribe women from Laos, who normally confine themselves to their own, tight-knit community and rarely venture more than

county health department gives free immunizations once a month at our Mother-Baby program. Many of the parents say they simply feel more comfortable coming to our program for shots than to a county clinic. And, yes, we serve around 80 moms each day, sometimes more.

In retrospect, I'd say all I had was good intentions. I wanted to get something off the ground, and I lacked ability, enormously. But I had good will, and because of the good will and the determination to do the job, the job got done. It didn't get done out of efficiency. I think if we'd stayed with the efficiency of the group of people we first met with, we'd be still sitting around the table, planning. We just jumped in and we did it, and it caught on from there.

Bill Sparks, the man who taught me all about diapers, also played a major role in getting the program off the ground. He was the first chairman of the Mother-Baby Advisory Board, and his wife, Marlene, was one of the first Mother-Baby mentors. In recognition of their efforts, and Bill's tremendous contribution to the growth of the Food Bank as a whole, we've named the program the Sparks Mother-Baby program.

His employment transfer to Ohio was a great loss to SFBS. I lost one of my dearest mentors, and the poor of Sacramento lost one of their strongest advocates.

blocks from their apartment complexes, have found in our classes a place where they feel welcomed and comfortable. In halting English, nods and smiles, they communicate warmly with moms whose native language is Spanish, Russian or English. Recently, the women have begun sharing ethnic dishes and cooking styles with their classmates. One week there was a class on making egg rolls, another week, tacos.

Today, three years after county officials told us our idea was essentially doomed, the

STARTING FROM SCRATCH

DENISE BRANDT WENT TO WORK AS A secretary for Father Madigan in May, 1992, shortly after getting a degree in psychology from California State University, Sacramento.

"Father Dan and the board members had been talking about a baby program for some time, but we'd just moved into the old grocery warehouse, and it hadn't gotten off the ground," she recalled.

In October, after the SFBS board meeting with officials from the county and health organizations, Brandt timidly approached Fr. Dan, saying she'd like to have a part in running the new program.

"I was afraid he'd laugh at me," she recalled. "I really knew nothing about starting a program, although I had ideas of what we should do." Instead, Fr. Dan asked Brandt to get the program off the ground, and told her he'd planned a grand opening in just two months!

"I thought, 'Are you out of your mind?'" Brandt recalled, laughing. "But we worked and worked for the next month and a half. We got about 20 really interested people, and from there picked a board. We had a credit with Raley's supermarket Food for Family's program, enough to buy formula for the first year. We wanted to be able to feed babies for three days, and provide 20 diapers to each baby for that period of time. At the time, no program in Sacramento was providing both food and diapers for babies.

"We really wanted to get in touch with the moms, so we could maybe make a difference in the lives of their children.

"I was so scared this wasn't going to happen, but with all these people's help, we had the grand opening and about 100 people were there. Instantly, it seemed, all of Sacramento got the word, and within a couple of months we were serving up to 100 babies a day, five days a week.

"I know that it really made a difference in some people's lives. Just to get a baby bed to a family whose infant was sleeping in a drawer. Or to give some advice to a teenaged mom who'd show up with a two-day-old baby from the hospital, not having any idea of what to do. Most of our volunteers were women who'd had children, so they were full of basic knowledge. It was really gratifying to be able to pass this knowledge on."

Now 29, Brandt runs the Mother-Baby program at SFBS' Del Paso Heights Food Locker.

NICOLASA

IT WAS A FEW DAYS BEFORE THANKSGIVING, 1995, and Nicolasa Ramirez had hit rock bottom. Her landlord had recently informed her that he needed to sell the four-bedroom tract house she and her six children share, paying reduced rent under the U.S. government's Section 8 subsidized rental program. Pushing her six-month-old daughter in a stroller and holding the hands of girls aged 4 and 3, she'd embarked on a discouraging hunt for another rental. One place was filthy and overpriced. Another's owner said her children would not be allowed to play in the back yard. Another flatly told her she had too many kids.

"Nobody wants six kids," Nicolasa said, her broad face scowling in frustration. It was beginning to look as if the family, having been homeless before, would once again be forced to live in cramped, cheap motels.

Instead of decorating her house for the holidays, Nicolasa began packing away nonessentials in boxes. Although she loves to cook, she says, for the first time she was too depressed and too broke to consider Thanksgiving dinner. She was dreading Christmas, and the spectre of no home and no presents for her children.

"I was so down, I couldn't even move," she recalls. "And you know, just then, Susan called, and said 'Come on down to the Mother-Baby program, Nicolasa, 'cause we have a turkey for you.' "

SFBS' Mother-Baby program and its director, Susan Bianchini, have provided a refuge and community for Nicolasa for three years, since the day she ran out of formula and diapers for her toddler, now five, and was referred to the program from the food line.

"They have classes to cook and to help be a better mother," she explains, earnestly. "I learn, like, don't yell at my kids, and that you don't have to buy new things to have some furniture in your house." She points proudly at a used couch, TV set and book-

shelf she found at rock-bottom prices by shopping at garage sales "in rich people's neighborhoods" – a tip from a thrifty shopping class at the Mother-Baby program. Displayed on a living room shelf is a row of hardcover books she bought at bargain prices at a garage sale. They include ponderous titles on geopolitics and history that Nicolasa realizes she will never read, but that she hopes will someday benefit her children. "Books are precious," she points out.

In addition to garage-sale thrift, Mother-Baby classes taught Nicolasa how to conserve on electricity (she sits in a dim living room with heavy curtains drawn, saving on both heating and lighting bills). Just as important as penny-pinching strategies are the social skills and self-awareness that have grown along with friendships made at Mother-Baby classes.

"I learned how to be a good friend – to speak how you really feel," she explains. "It feels good going there, because the people are always smiling with you."

The classes and informal waiting-room chats at the Mother-Baby program were the first time she had ever been encouraged to speak her mind, said Nicolasa, 29. "I learn little by little that first you have to accept yourself, then you can be a better parent," she says. "If you really want support in giving up old ways and being a better person, they are always there for you."

Nicolasa is a fiercely protective mother, proudly pointing out that "I am always with my kids." While other teens in her neighborhood are having babies or dying in gang fights, she says, her 15-year-old son is busy painting and fixing up their house or practicing football. Her 12-year-old daughter still plays with dolls.

In addition to getting a three-day supply of diapers and formula for her baby once a month at the program, Nicolasa takes her children there for free immunizations and comes home with laundry soap.

More important to Nicolasa than the products, she says, is the sense of community and acceptance she's come to depend upon at the program. Nobody there judges her harshly because her marriage is plagued by frequent separations, or she doesn't have the money to buy many of the things her children want. Instead, she has found friends there who have encouraged her to have confidence and stand up for herself in her relationships.

When her sixth child was born, a new acquaintance from a Mother-Baby class took a bus to Nicolasa's house, where she spent the day cleaning and cooking for Nicolasa's other children so she could enjoy rest and time with her infant.

"When I first started going to Mother-Baby, I was afraid they would turn me away," she says. "I was wrong."

"You don't have programs like that free anymore," Nicolasa says. "They take care of your kids and they have all the patience, sometimes with 40 kids in there! One day I was thinking, 'What's gonna happen if they close one day here?' I was thinking maybe

one day I'm gonna have a lot of money and I will help them stay open."

For now, Nicolasa is giving back by helping to interpret classes for Spanish-speaking clients, and by offering her own class in both Spanish and English: How to Cook Enchiladas.

The Mother-Baby program salvaged Nicolasa's Thanksgiving, giving her family a turkey and all the trimmings. Volunteers later gave her a Christmas tree and decorations. A couple of weeks before Christmas, Nicolasa boarded a bus with other mothers and children involved in the Mother-Baby program, and was taken down the Sacramento River Delta to St. Joseph's Church in Clarksburg. There the children were visited by Santa Claus, who brought gifts especially for them to put under their Christmas trees.

And when the family got home, she got the best news of all — her landlord decided to take his house off the market to spare Nicolasa and her children from homelessness.

"You know, there are a lot of people outside that love us. They worry about us," Nicolasa says. "It makes me cry sometimes, and I always pray for them."

DIANE & TRACI

Just a few steps away from the food line, the Mother-Baby program has a decidedly more inviting, familial atmosphere. Mothers must still check in at the front desk, where Director Susan Bianchini greets them warmly and checks them off on a computer file.

The soundtrack from "Winnie the Pooh" mingles with children's chatter in the tiny playroom. A plastic, child-sized kitchen and tool shop line one wall and children and toys are crowded together on the floor. Moms sit on two facing couches, waiting to be called for a session with a volunteer mentor.

On the wall are two hand-painted rainbows, one with the names of each color printed in English, the other in Spanish. Down the hall are two small offices where volunteer mentors meet with the mothers (or, occasionally, fathers or grandparents) who have come for a three-day supply of diapers, baby formula and food.

The mentors' desks are covered with cans of formula, boxes of baby cereal, vitamins and jars of mashed fruits and vegetables —

visual aids for the many clients who speak little or no English. Flyers printed in Spanish, English, Russian and Lao explain the program guidelines, and invite clients to a free immunization clinic once each month.

Volunteer Diane Yamane, 28, offers her client a chair across from the desk. Traci, 23, has come to the Mother-Baby program early in January for diapers and formula for her 7-month old son. Although her husband has a steady job at a tire store, the couple sometimes has a hard time making it through the month with Traci staying at home and drawing meager unemployment checks.

"Most people have a tough time at the end of the month," Traci tells Diane, also the mother of a baby boy. "For me, it's that last week of the month to the middle of the first week. That's when I have problems.

"Rent's due, and all the bills are due, and by then you've run out of all of your WIC (federally-subsidized) formula, and it's like, now what?"

Traci, a plump blonde woman in flowered stretch pants and a sweat shirt, says she learned about Mother-Baby through the food stamp program. "We were making $40 over the limit for getting food stamps, but you know, $40 doesn't make all that much of difference when you're looking at $70 to $100 in food."

Traci says she's excited, because this afternoon she has an interview for a job as supervisor at a preschool.

"I'm not really ready to go back to work — I hate the idea of leaving my baby all day —

but my husband's income just doesn't cut it," she explains. "I was looking for part-time, but a lot of the daycares and preschools want as much as they pay you to work. It just doesn't pay. Even though I have two year's of college and eight year's experience, it's hard finding a job for more than $6 an hour. You can be a manager at Burger King for more than that."

Diane nods supportively. "It's a shame how government's set up, so where if you work but don't make very much, you don't qualify for some of the benefits you need."

"Oh, we won't get food stamps if I get this job," Traci says. "And I won't *need* to come here. I told my husband, if I don't have to go, I'm not gonna go, because I don't feel I should come here and take something somebody else should be using."

Diane asks what kind of formula the baby drinks, and checks "soy" on the client form.

"How about powdered milk?" Diane asks. "A lot of people don't like the taste, but mixed into pancakes or mashed potatoes — it's great for that." Traci accepts, and asks for cereal and medium-sized diapers. Diane shows her a list of classes for the month: infant massage, stress reduction, self esteem, Lao cooking and basic nutrition. Mother-Baby clients must take at least one class every six weeks to participate in the program.

"Stress reduction," Traci says. "I could use that."

Diane wishes her luck on the interview, and sends her with her form to a stock room down the hall where her order will be filled.

Added to the diapers, formula and cereal

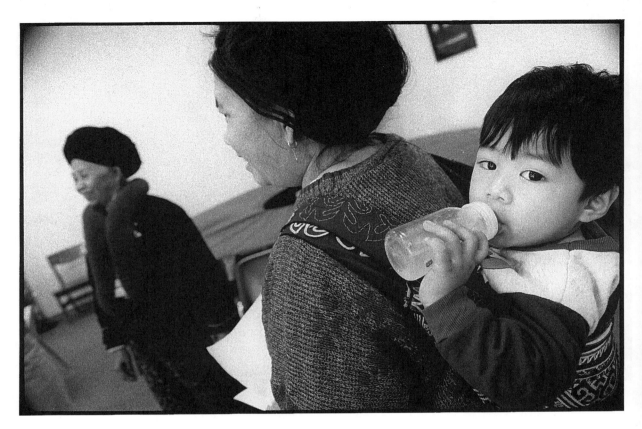

this day are extra donated items: baby shampoo and lotion, a stuffed toy and some hotel-sized toiletries for Traci.

"That was a good one," Diane says when Traci has gone. "It feels good giving a hand to people who are willing to help themselves. There are those that seem to have no incentive to get out of the system, like this girl I saw yesterday with four kids, all with different dads. That's depressing."

For every client like Traci or Nicolasa, there is one that is abusive or abused, drug-addicted or caught in a cycle of repeated pregnancies with no husband and no job, mentors say.

A woman once brought in one of her ten grandchildren, explaining the baby didn't look healthy because she was exhibiting the symptoms of her mother's crack addiction. All nine of the baby's siblings were also crack babies, all with different fathers.

"We have a lot of homeless families, and it gets really disconcerting, knowing there is only so much you can do," says volunteer Katie Kuhn, a retired medical office manager. "So I go through my house, and my daughter and her kids go through their house, and we gather all the toys and books and clothes that we can, and everyone in the family feels like they can help, if only a little."

Volunteers refer troubled parents to counselors, shelters, drug treatment and job training programs. Often the mothers have fine parenting skills, but poverty has forced them to live in substandard housing. Mentors who hear tales of rent-gouging slum-lords, or cold-water apartments with broken appliances, refer clients to Legal Aid for help with tenants' rights. Occasionally, mentors are compelled to report an abusive or neglectful parent to child welfare authorities.

"If children look as if they're not being well cared for, we'll turn them in," says volunteer Sunny Mahoney, a mother of five grown, successful children. "Unfortunately, social services are so overwhelmed, they don't respond until a file gets rather thick."

Mahoney says she appreciates her experiences as a mentor, because they keep her from being insulated in the comforts of her middle-class neighborhood. "You just feel so grateful for your own life," she says. "Sometimes I think, 'God, how can you give people so many problems?'"

She sadly recalls the visit of a sullen young mother and her angry toddler.

"He was just tearing the place apart – hitting people, destroying toys and really being incorrigible. When I told his mother she would have to control her child, she just shrugged and said, 'Call the police. I can't control him.'"

As the mother and son left the building, however, one of the mentors saw the boy's shoe was untied. She approached him, gave him a hug, tied his shoe, then gave him another hug. "Suddenly, this boy started behaving like a sweet little puppy," Mahoney recalled. "It was so obvious that what he needed was love."

Volunteer Kuhn has been a Mother-Baby program mentor since the program began, and says the rewards outweigh the frustrations. "There really is a feeling of love here," she says.

Like many volunteers, Kuhn has devised a coping strategy for handling the occasional clients who are rude, demanding, or apparently unwilling to try for a better life.

"I try to step back," Kuhn says. "I think, 'Hey, maybe they've got more problems than I can even imagine.'"

Bridge Builder Leotha Sullivan

USING ALL OUR ASSETS

SENIOR BRIDGE BUILDERS

MARCH 1993

Dear Friends:

Sacramento Food Bank Services is now 18 years old. It provides food, clothing, housing, literacy, and mother-baby care to people. SFBS owes its ongoing existence to generous folks like yourself. We have hundreds of volunteers and thousands of donors. And while you wonderful people come from all ages, races and religions, the majority of you are children of the Great Depression.

Senior citizens – your deep concern and genuine love is so very uplifting to the unfortunate people at the other side of the window. Albert Schweitzer once said that those who have been hurt always carry the scar of that hurt with them. He claims that because of hurt, people are drawn close to others who are suffering. He calls it, "the brotherhood of those who bear the mark of pain." I often think that the experience of the Great Depression was a mixed blessing as it fostered such sterling qualities of charity in you.

The establishing of senior citizen groups at the churches of Sacred Heart and Immaculate Conception has certainly paid off for me. I gave you folks an organizational machine. You give SFBS many volunteer hours, much revenue mentoring time. That's why I am renovating appropriate space and making plans for the putting together of a senior group called "The Senior Bridge Builders."

This new club will not treat senior people like fragile china. It will not offer pacifying, catering or accommodating programs. It will not indulge in stitchery, ceramics, macrame or flower arranging. Instead, it will be a club where experienced people meet, enjoy good food, good speakers, good recreation and most important of all, get their teeth into some very worthwhile projects.

This club will fly under the banner of the statement made by Cicero almost 2,000 years ago: "Age is truly respectable in the man who guards himself from becoming the property of others, indicates his just right and maintains his proper authority to the last moments of his life." May God bless you for being a SFBS supporter.

With every good wish,

Fr. Dan Madigan

Dear Friends:

This letter is primarily for people my own age and older. "Golden age," "senior citizens," "rest homes" and even "retirement" were alien words to me as a youngster. Then, additional years brought additional respect and venerability. Death was the only force that removed one from the stage of life.

Now all is changed. Our sophisticated society moves one quickly from life's stage. Impersonalization has taken over. Individual interaction is pushed into the background.

This mass-production, conveyor-belt living system of ours needs to be looked at. People need to be seen rather than the crowd. St. Francis' advice, "Grant that I may not so much seek to be understood as to understand," needs to be put into action.

Yes, we need to slow down. We need to smell the roses. *We need to build bridges.* We need to see to it that differences of race, creed, sex or religion make no difference to us. Please study the poem outlined below. It will be one of the mottoes for our new Bridge Builders Club.

The Bridge Builders

An old man traveling a lone highway,

Came at the evening cold and gray,

To a chasm vast and deep and wide,

Through which was flowing a sullen tide.

The old man crossed in the twilight dim,

The sullen stream held no fears for him;

But he turned when safe on the other side,

And built a bridge to span the tide.

"Old man," cried a fellow pilgrim near,

"You're wasting your time in building here.

Your journey will end with the closing day;

You never again will pass this way.

You have crossed the chasm deep and wide,

Why build you this bridge at eventide?"

The builder lifted his old gray head:

"Good friend, in the path I have come," he said.

"There followeth after me today

youth whose feet must pass this way,

This stream which has been as naught to me

To that fair-haired youth may pitfall be;

He, too, must cross in the twilight dim –

Good friend, I am building this bridge for him."

Will Allen Dromgoole

With every good wish,

Fr. Dan Madigan

Dear Friends:

I was raised in a family with two parents, four brothers and four sisters. Our family was not run by a committee. Neither were our family rules drawn up by consensus. Mom and Dad were clearly in charge. Mom was the vocal leader. Dad was the quieter partner.

Now while both my parents were gentle, kind and loving they were nevertheless far removed from being wishy-washy. We kids always knew where we stood with them. Conduct standards were well defined. Accountability demanded. Daily workload expected to be accomplished. Laziness unaccepted. And aspirations always encouraged.

Harry Truman said leadership is getting people to do things they don't want to do. If this is so then my mom was a Napoleon.

General Mark Clark said leadership is walking the extra mile. And if this is true my dad was a Mother Teresa of Calcutta.

Grandparents and great-grandparents, you are remarkable people. You lived through history's Great Depression. You have a tremendous amount of knowledge in your head. Much love in your heart. Great values in your system. All younger generations need to hear from you.

Grandparents, great-grandparents, you are not over the hill. You have lots and lots to offer. I need your help in the putting together of our new Bridge Builders program.

Please give me a call.

With every good wish,

Fr. Dan Madigan

I CAME TO THE UNITED STATES 30 YEARS ago

from a culture where all age groups were treated much the same,

with perhaps the elderly persons having a little edge on the others.

Incapacity, senility and disengagement were unknown concepts in our

community. From cradle to grave, a person's life was lived out in the open for

everyone to see. No one ever suggested institutionalization to the elderly person.

People grew old in their own family environment and, with the years, received added respect.

Everyone grasped the absurdity of life clearly, recognizing as factual that tragedy, sorrow
and death were part of man's lot and that, as Robert Lowell put it, "Age is the bilge we
cannot shake from the mop."

I therefore found it difficult to accept this country's lack of respect for the venerability of old age. The national preoccupation with youth amazed me, as did the money, time and energy spent in the effort to stay physically fit and wrinkle-free. At the same time, I saw a pitiless disregard for the aged. I saw public indifference to their pauperization by inflationary costs; to the cruelly insensitive treatment reported in rest home care; and to the emotional trauma of the active retiree who finds himself "put out to pasture," a societal reject.

Moved by the seniors' plight, I began my study and research into their multitudinous problems. As a graduate student in social work and as a pastor, I've tried to understand and bring services to the elderly urban poor.

My experience studying community-based adult activity centers influenced my thinking and vision. I learned that seniors did not want to be amused, pacified or catered to. They resented being made the passive recipients of attention and were not blind to the fact that many of their programs had created new careers, not for them, but for the managers and program directors of senior centers.

At Immaculate Conception Church in 1977, I invited senior parishioners to form a self-directed group that would bypass the stitchery-ceramics-macrame approach to group involvement. What emerged was a group of totally alive people who were a powerhouse of encouragement and strength to each other. Essentially, the group got to-gether to socialize, but out of these get-togethers grew a sense of belonging and an opportunity to do meaningful volunteer work.

Around the same time I had a more ambitious idea, aimed at truly building bridges between the young and old in our community, and making use of the generosity of middle-class parishioners to create a housing project for the elderly urban poor. The building of the Ellis Senior Residence, and its eventual failure, taught me how truly difficult it is to fulfill those ambitions, and how far we have yet to go in building those bridges.

When I arrived at Immaculate Conception Church, I "inherited" an entire complex that covered nearly a city block. It included an active elementary school, a vacant 30-room convent, the church and a rectory that once housed five priests. At the early part of the century, these buildings were the center of the Catholic community in Sacramento. The school, in its heyday, was a real academy of learning. Nuns who lived in the convent taught not only the basic subjects but drama, music and fine arts. By 1976, however, the convent was empty, and the academy was struggling as a typical inner-city grade school.

It seemed a travesty, an inexcusable waste, for this beautiful brick convent to sit vacant in an area crying out for services. Why couldn't we refurbish it into housing for the elderly poor? It seemed that doing so might serve two great purposes. We could

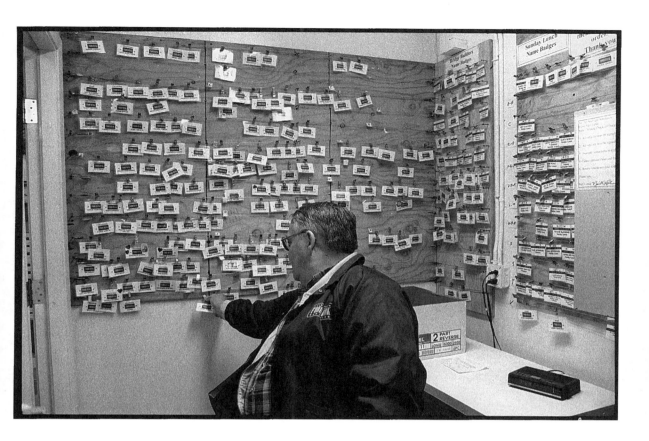

provide much needed housing in a safe, affordable setting for isolated seniors. And we could build bridges between the young and old. The seniors in the housing program could provide a "school of wisdom" for the students in the school of learning next door.

City housing authorities were not encouraging. They insisted that to qualify for any grants from them, we would have to gut the interior of the building, redesign stairwells and relocate walls and windows. But my parishioners were behind the project, and we got start-up funding from a private foundation. After initial construction work was done, several couples from the parish "adopted" bedrooms in the old convent to paint, decorate and furnish. Many of these volunteers were middle and upper-middle-class people with tremendous taste, and the

rooms were decorated beautifully. The common dining room was furnished with a lovely table and fine china, and throughout the new congregate living facility were lovely decorator's touches. In retrospect, we overdid it.

On opening day, there was a huge celebration and open house at the Ellis Residence, named after the parish's first two pastors, Fathers William and John Ellis. Visitors were amazed to see that the standards of the residence were such that any middle-class person would be comfortable bringing a parent to live there. In fact, the first group of people to move in were refined, well-educated people on fixed incomes. We quickly encountered two problems. Because the building was in a poor neighborhood, the middle-class children of these residents felt

uncomfortable and somewhat embarrassed about their parents being there. At the same time, the over-decoration of the house, and the social caliber of its first residents, inadvertently excluded the very people I had intended would benefit from the residence. The poor, uneducated seniors felt very uncomfortable there after a very short time and left, returning to isolated life in downtown residence hotels. The residence was nearly always under-occupied, despite its reasonable cost of around $300 a month for rent, meals and utilities. When I left the parish, after ten years of operation, the Ellis Residence closed down.

The Ellis Residence also provided a lesson on how difficult it is to bring generational mixing back into this society. We worked with Bishop Manogue High School students on developing a program of regular visitation of the seniors at Ellis. We hoped to develop continuing relationships between the generations. But what we ran into was kids with not enough time, matched with seniors with too much time. The students had after-school sports, music lessons, boyfriends, part-time jobs and dances. Within a short time, it became apparent this project, too, would fail to meet expectations.

The Ellis Residence experience tells me how difficult it truly is to build bridges between generations and especially between the social classes. So often great results fall short of great intentions. It is so much easier to be filled with the spirit of giving than to actually fill our hours with those who need our gifts. We are more comfortable handing services through a window – keeping the poor "in their place" – than working beside them as they climb their own ladders to better their lives.

The Ellis Residence may have ultimately failed, but generosity of spirit among the seniors in our community thrives. The group of seniors at Immaculate Conception parish formed the backbone of SFBS as our programs grew in the past two decades, inspiring seniors from other parishes to become involved as well.

It was this group of involved seniors that inspired the idea of a Bridge Builders organization at SFBS. Why not invite seniors from throughout the community to become involved with each other and the satisfying volunteer opportunities at the Food Bank? We ask our Bridge Builders to donate four volunteer hours each week to the program of their choice at the Food Bank. Many have worked in several capacities, trying on jobs until they find one that "fits." Some retired people make themselves available at a moment's notice to pick up canned goods, address envelopes or provide vacation relief. In acknowledgement of their service, we host a monthly Bridge Builders' luncheon with a speaker. The Bridge Builders themselves plan outings and bus trips to places like Reno and Hearst Castle. Program Director Dorothee Mull seems tireless in organizing all the details of this vital part of SFBS.

I think it is no coincidence that so many of those who are most active as volunteers are of the generation that lived through the Depression. The Depression sensitized people. I often wonder, when those who lived through the Depression are gone, will the people after them be as sensitive to the poor?

Seniors are also among our most loyal donors. In notes that arrive with checks for $10 or $15, I hear the sense of responsibility for others. "This is all I can afford now," an elderly donor might explain, or, "My nephew is having problems with his family, so I have to help him out a little now and can't send as much as I want." The concern and sacrifice is very humbling.

LEOTHA SULLIVAN

"I'M A CALL GIRL," SAYS LEOTHA SULLIVAN, laughing. "Whenever Dorothee calls, I come," she says referring to Program Director Dorothee Mull. Sullivan, a retired telephone operator and mother of three grown children, is one of the club's most dedicated volunteers.

"Bridge Builders is definitely a way for people to feel useful," she says. "You can always lift your hand at doing something at the Food Bank – many, many projects. The Bridge Builders brings all of the volunteers together in a social group, and it rewards them with a luncheon.

"It's a sense of belonging," says Sullivan, who is widowed. "I walk in over there at the Food Bank, and by golly, I can't even walk through the halls without going, `hello, hello, hello.'"

Instead of signing up for a regular four-hour-a-week shift, she works "at all the little extra things that somebody else isn't assigned or can't do," Sullivan says.

Sullivan's late husband, George, was the first president of their parish senior group, and when Bridge Builders was first conceived, she served on its board.

"I'm sure Father Dan had our parish senior group in mind when he started Bridge Builders," Sullivan says. "We're a solid group. I don't think you'll find a more mixed group anywhere – all nationalities, all types. We're drawn together because we're a group that helps and cares."

It was Leotha Sullivan who convinced board members at their first meeting they had nothing to lose by participating in Macy's department store "benefit shopping day" as a fundraiser for the food bank. Tickets were $10, all of which went to SFBS, and they entitled the donor entrance to Macy's on a day of bargains set aside for the ticket holders.

"We sold about 6,000 tickets, winning the first prize – $8,000 – for most tickets sold," Sullivan recalls. "So we put in our treasury right from the word go, the very first year, $14,000."

Empowered by that success, the Bridge Builders volunteered for other fundraising efforts, from mailing 6,000 newsletters each month to doing set-up, staffing and cleanup of major fundraising events. At the annual Saca Ball, one of SFBS' most important fundraisers, Bridge Builders provide many hours in sending invitations, setting up and staffing tables and cleaning up. Ilham and Tony Saca, owners of Filco appliance and electronics stores, hold this fundraiser, generously donating the use of their home, providing the catering and spending many hours on arrangements for this event. Last year, the Saca Ball netted $112,000 for SFBS.

Sullivan is among the workers at the Saca Ball and at dozens of other Bridge Builders activities.

"I'm fortunate, because I can do many things," she says. "I can drive, thank God, and I can be in public or behind the scenes. If I can serve, that's what I want to do."

LYNN AND LEIGHTON HATCH

LYNN HATCH HAD BEEN WORKING REGULARLY at the Food Bank window for six years when one day she walked into Father Dan's office and said, "I can't do it anymore."

"I think I was becoming jaded," she explains. "The final blow was when a client got very angry with a gal I worked with every Tuesday, and hit her in the head with a two-by-four. She had to have six stitches in her head. I said, `Maybe it's time for someone fresher.' I didn't like myself for feeling that way, and now, three years later, I think I could go back to it. But at the time, I just didn't feel safe. I no longer had the heart for it."

"Loving the unlovable is pretty severe," added Lynn's husband, retired Sacramento County Superior Court Judge Leighton Hatch. "It takes tremendous patience. It's easy to love the people in Bridge Builders, for example, but when you really see the sometimes ugly, profane types...it takes a lot of effort."

Lynn and Leighton Hatch had both put in many hours at SFBS when Father Dan asked them to be co-chairpersons of the new Bridge Builders board. Judge Hatch is one of 13 community leaders on the SFBS Advisory Board. In addition to Lynn's work at the window, the Hatches have mentored several clients of the Havens Transitional Housing program, making weekly visits to their homes and helping out with budgeting, housekeeping and job skills.

Judge Hatch, who is frequently called out

of retirement to sit as a judge in Northern California courts, is the master of ceremonies at Bridge Builders luncheons, and both the Hatches have served on the board for three years.

SFBS "has made us more aware of the needs in our community, certainly," Leighton Hatch says. Having seen firsthand from the bench the end result of children brought up in fatherless homes troubled by drugs, alcohol and poor education, he said, "this work attempts to alleviate some of that."

"We judges live in kind of a cloistered atmosphere," Hatch says. "You get so focused on sustaining this objection, or ruling on that. It's very structured." Working on "the other end," which is often chaotic, he says, "gives a little balance to my profession."

TED & JOAN BOUGHTON

LIKE MANY OF THE BRIDGE BUILDERS, TED AND Joan Boughton have been involved in a variety of SFBS programs, from serving as literacy tutors and mentors to formerly homeless families to planning speakers for Bridge Builders luncheons. Ted Boughton, a retired trailer salesman, and Joan, mother of five grown children and grandmother of seven, said they donate time and money to SFBS because "of all the programs around, you know that whatever you give is going directly back into the programs."

The couple lives in the neat South Sacramento ranch style home where they raised their children. It is several miles from the Food Bank, but they make the drive rou-

tinely to put in hours at what they jokingly refer to as the "no brainer" job of monitoring the door and sign-up sheet. They also make themselves available to pick up food or work on the mailing committee that sends out thousands of letters at a time.

After working in the Food Locker for several years, Joan Boughton tutored a young mother who had dropped out of school when her mother died and never learned to read.

Ted and Joan have taken Havens clients to court appearances, helped them find jobs and "adopted" large families for gift-giving at Christmastime. Like other mentors, they've helped provide to clients the type of networking opportunities enjoyed by the middle-class, but out of reach for the poor.

The Boughtons also serve on the Bridge Builders Board of Directors.

"We've had the same board for three years – nobody wants off, we enjoy each other so much!" said Joan.

"Bridge Builders is a great source of volunteers because we all have the time," Joan said, "and some members work like dogs for the organization. Father Dan has a tremendously loyal following. He's such a hard worker himself, I think he expects that of everyone. And people come through because they see he's not all talk. I mean, what's been accomplished is amazing, really. The expanse of it!"

In addition to providing an enjoyable social outlet through Bridge Builders, the Boughtons' experiences at SFBS have expanded their concept about "the other half" they serve as volunteers.

"I think it's given me and Joan, too, an appreciation of the problems of the poor," said Ted. "I knew about them, but I had never been associated with them."

"I think we realized, too," said Joan, "that just though they're homeless doesn't mean they are indolent or that they are just living off the freeway. I mean, these are families or mothers who all of a sudden have no money. They don't have a job, they have no money. So where do they live?"

Although they are Republicans, Joan said firmly, "I am *for* AFDC for people. Like my student, Rita. She could not exist without it, and she's not abusing it. She's very cautious with her five children, none of them have ever been in any trouble, and she needs the help."

"I guess maybe I'd have more of a chip on my shoulder with regard to welfare," were it not for her work with SFBS, Joan said. "You know, 'this welfare business, why don't they clean it up?' But I think people on AFDC truly need AFDC, and they don't need these cuts they're putting through. Like Rita. She's not able to pay the utilities!"

Added Ted, "I'm sure some welfare recipients are riding along just for the welfare, but some are really trying to dig themselves out, and it's remarkable."

Recycling Program Director Philip Stoakley

COMPLETING THE CIRCLE

RECYCLING PROGRAM

SEPTEMBER 1991

Dear Friends:

I feel that our priorities today are completely out of whack. And I feel that if you meditate on the following facts for a while you will agree with me.

The movie "Terminator 2" cost $70 million to produce. The average major league baseball player's salary is $900,000 annually. Boxers are given as high as $30 million to step into the ring. Our country is Four Trillion dollars in debt. One out of every five of our children grows up in poverty. Twenty-five percent of our teenagers drop out of school. Ten million U.S. people live on the edge of homelessness. Thirty-seven million families have no medical insurance.

Yes indeed, it's because our priorities are all topsy-turvy that our great nation is now producing two countries, one working and productive, one depressed and hopeless.

So, my friends, the days are long gone when we can afford to be passive recipients. We have to stand up and say our piece and say it loudly.

With every good wish,

Fr. Dan Madigan

Dear Friends:

My mom loved Mr. and Mrs. O'Connell. They taught her in the little two-room rural school house she attended. They were truly her mentors.

A classmate of my Mom's once handed Mrs. O'Connell a rather valuable coin. This youngster claimed she found it under a rock. In the presence of the class Mrs. O'Connell cross-examined this child. The little girl said she removed a rock from the footpath that led from the school to its outdoor latrine. Mrs. O'Connell asked why she removed this rock. The child said she did so because she considered it a hazard. Mrs. O'Connell complimented the little girl on her goodness, then explained to all the class that it was indeed herself who put the coin there. She also explained that her purpose in doing so was to see who would remove the rock. Then she handed the coin back to the little Good Samaritan and said, "Spend this on yourself."

On a visit to Ireland some years ago, I was told of the tragic death of one of my boyhood friends. Eamon Walsh was returning from town. It was a very cold day, and he was all bundled up. He was driving his farm tractor, and didn't see the large stone in the middle of the narrow road. His front tire hit it and his tractor overturned. Eamon was killed instantly. At his funeral a few of our neighbors felt very bad. They had passed by that stone. They did not do what my mom's little friend did. They did not remove the hazard.

Friends, life has lots of hazards and pitfalls for all of us. We should try to remove them for each other. It's just the right thing to do.

May 1993 be a Happy New Year for you. May God reward you with great peace of mind. And may He assist you in the daily developing and enlarging of that kind heart of yours.

With every good wish,

Fr. Dan Madigan

Dear Friends:

When I was a youngster life was quite simple and easy going. When shopping, people carried handbags for groceries, tin cans for lamp oil, bottles for milk, earthenware jars for Guinness and their radio batteries for recharging.

As I grew older, I saw the proliferation of paper goods, cardboard boxes, styrofoam cups and plastic containers descend upon us with the vengeance of an avalanche. However today, and thank God for it, I am seeing the return of a philosophy of reducing, reusing and recycling.

Our SFBS recycling program is doing well, thanks to the great support we are receiving from many of my fellow pastors, schools and business acquaintances. At the rate things are happening we will, in the very near future, be in need of a rather large warehouse. Perhaps one of you dear readers and good friends may be able to help us with this. If so, please contact me right away.

With every good wish,

Fr. Dan Madigan

Dear Friends:

My 20-year journey from church basement to a sprawling, three-building service center has taught me a great deal about food, administration, volunteers, fundraising, computers, refrigeration, trucks, vans, trailers and forklifts. I have also learned about human failure, power failure and food spoilage. But above all, the years have taught me how complex the nature of poverty can be.

Poverty stretches all the way from mere shortage to total destitution. The same is true of the people who come to us for help. It is a mistake to classify the disadvantaged. To assume that they are cheaters, loafers and chiselers is an outrage. A diversity of people from all ages, creeds and colors come to our food outlets. Derelicts, winos and street people stand in the long lines with the mentally ill, the drug addicts, the prostitutes. We find there, too, the totally unskilled, the illiterate and the unemployable.

Others are physically handicapped, chronically ill, socially stunted or far along in years. But the frightening fact is this: The majority of those who come to us look and act like ourselves. They are local, neighborhood folk — moms and dads who have run out of money because their meager income, be it welfare or minimum wage, is not enough to live on. Many need help with money management or job seeking skills. Some never learned to read.

Today, Sacramento Food Bank Services continues to build its program of mentoring, job training and recycling. People with successful lives are sharing the good fortune of their education and solid upbringing with people who have had only bad breaks. As we recycle materials to save resources and support our programs, every one of us involved with SFBS is also on a personal recycling mission. Some are recycling their lives to overcome addictions and poverty and learn job skills. Volunteers are working to become more patient, more generous. It seems as if we are still on the mountainside, but some days we can see the top.

With every good wish,

Fr. Dan Madigan

I GREW UP IN THE LITTLE VILLAGE of
Shanagolden, County Limerick. We could walk down to the
Shannon River and the town of Foynes, where aviation history was
made. The first Flying Boat – Pan American Airway's luxurious Yankee
Clipper, landed there in the river the year after I was born (1939). I remember as
a very young child watching these astonishing flying ships land in the river, and being
amazed at the happy, tanned, exotic looking people disembark.

Americans – movie stars, businessmen, high-level diplomats. From the age of five, I
decided I wanted to go to wherever these people were from.

The Yankee Clipper brought not only my earliest fantasies of America, but my first glimpse of a custom that was totally foreign to us. It was a custom that would only begin to really take hold in the U.S. after World War II, but those wealthy Americans brought a taste of it down from the sky and into the village of Foynes: waste. Canned goods, something we just never saw, were consumed in the flying boat and at the Inn where the travelers stayed. And when the cans were thrown away, they became our treasure. What a perfect little container for boiling eggs! We'd each one of us have a can and boil our own eggs in it, thinking it was the cleverest thing to ever come along.

The most vivid memories I have of my Mom and my sisters in those years were of them sitting and darning socks in the evening. It was one example of the kind of frugal practicality that was our way of life. There was no such thing as disposability or waste. You didn't buy anything except what you couldn't barter, and what was truly essential. We produced our own milk, our own meat, and used or gave to our neighbors every edible piece. Even the intestines of a hog were used to make a sausage we called "blood pudding." And because we didn't have a funnel with which to stuff the sausage casing, we made one. Just take a bottle, fill it with boiling water about a quarter of the way up. You do that several times, then plunge the bottle into a tub of cold water. Didn't the bottle break evenly, right at the line of the boiling water? Then we'd sand the glass a bit, and there you'd have it – a funnel.

There were only a couple of automobiles in our village when I was growing up, and only about 200 people. So when my father somehow got hold of an old automobile tire he was thrilled – new shoe soles for everyone in the family! We weren't very proud of those tire-soled shoes, in fact a bit ashamed. Now here I am today, delighted with my expensive Birkenstocks and those same tire soles.

The women in our family shopped with baskets they had made from bulrushes. When I went off to school, my mother always insisted I carry a bottle of milk. We had no corks, so I made a cork out of newspaper, tightly folded to fit the bottle top. Each day I'd come home, scrub out the milk bottle for the next day, and make a new cork. Recycling was such a way of life we didn't have a word for it. You simply made every possible use of what you had, repaired and reused what was broken, and found new uses for things rather than discarding them.

Even Irish Coffee was born of this philosophy, right in the town of Foynes, in the pursuit of pleasing the wealthy American travelers. One day it was freezing when the Yankee Clipper passengers landed at Foynes Jetty, and they all headed shivering over to the first pub they saw. "Do you have anything hot?" one asked the barkeeper, Dempsey. Well, like all of us, he was quite limited in what he had. Other than Guinness, he had whisky, and he had coffee, and a little cream. So he told them he had coffee, poured a shot of whisky in it,

whipped up the cream and put in some of that. The travelers drank it.

"Is this Brazilian coffee?" one asked. "Hell, no, man," Dempsey responded. "It's Irish coffee!"

In those days, even graves were recycled. We buried our neighbors ourselves, in simple wooden caskets that would disintegrate. No cement-lined graves and $2,000 air-tight mahogany and steel caskets. No mention on the side of the casket of the gauge of steel used, as if it were a shotgun instead of a box for a body.

I can remember specifically burying an old lady, old Katie, and digging up her grave eight or nine years afterward to bury her brother. That was considered the thing to do. Leave Katie there, but there's nothing left of Katie, so bury her brother above her. Generations of families would be buried this way, and the families would take care of the graves, and nowhere would there be vast acres of cement-lined, forever unusable land given over to our refusal to accept the reality of death. A hundred years from now, who is going to maintain these places?

When I got to this country I was appalled at the waste, the excess packaging, the notion that disposable was better. When I saw discarded cans, I remembered what treasures we once thought they were.

When our Food Locker first started back at Immaculate Conception in Oak Park, we learned about recycling by trial and error.

for recycling. I'm too frugal to think that there was something going out of our buildings that could be turned into money. Obviously if somebody was coming and picking it up and it was valuable to them, why shouldn't it be income to us? But I was constantly reminded by a few of our people that it wasn't really worth our while — in the long run, we'd be spending more in labor hours than we could collect from recycling. But I thought that was wrong. Why couldn't we get a program off the ground to make recycling profitable, and use it to help recycle the lives of some of the people who come to us for help?

People would bring in bags of aluminum cans and place them next to a bin we had for newspapers. I'd be awakened at night by cans whirling around, dancing and clattering on the concrete in the wind. So we built two bins, one for cans and another for newspapers, and people would steal the cans. Then we devised a bin with a slot for depositing the cans, but no easy access for removing them. The newspaper truck grew to a great 18-wheeler, which served the dual purpose of recycling and providing sleeping quarters for several homeless men.

The recycling of newspapers and aluminum cans was fairly lucrative for our inner-city school, and we finally got the system down to where it wasn't creating a mess. A few years later, it really bothered me when I learned someone was coming to our food lockers to collect our cardboard

For years, I've been asked why I don't encourage the people in our food lines to volunteer in our programs. Even Bishop Quinn suggested that if Mr. So-and-So showed up in the line it meant he had no job, and that therefore we should give him a job volunteering. I strongly disagree with that philosophy, and it is one of the very few areas in which I guess I'm more conservative than many others on my board.

I believe our volunteers must have "mentor-ability," the ability to demonstrate and model to others such skills as reliability and responsibility. Through no fault of their own, most of the people in our food lines don't have those skills. That's not a condescension, it's just reality. What we ought to give to them, instead of the opportunity to volunteer, is real training for real jobs under responsible leadership. With training, supervision and exposure to a workplace that insists upon integrity and responsibility, people can transform their lives. We do them no favors handing them a salary but leaving them untrained.

I've seen what happens when a bureaucracy tries to employ the disadvantaged but doesn't follow through with caring supervision. Last summer, I went to a government agency where a number of older teenagers were employed temporarily in minimum wage jobs. We needed immediate help in loading a truck with some government surplus property we had just received. The young men were within yards of us, gathered around an outside patio table, but the man in charge of this bureaucracy did not seem to have the authority to go over and make them help us load. So my program director, dressed in a sports coat and tie, and the director of the agency itself, dressed likewise, and me, dressed as a priest, did the lifting as these kids just sat there and watched. It never even occurred to them to help or, if it did, they were plainly unwilling to do so.

It seemed everyone participating in that program was playing a game. These young people were brought in, paid a salary, got away with doing little or nothing, got no leadership, no training, and they walked away from that program with no skills and a modest amount of cash. I believe they left as lesser human beings, courtesy of the government.

There's a grave injustice done to people who are not supervised. You don't get people who are homeless and unemployed in order to get free or cheap labor done. You get them to train them. And if they're not wanting and willing and ready to be trained, then the whole thing has no purpose.

In our program, we're recycling attitudes. Not only do we hire people, we train them. We insist on reliability and integrity. We give them lots of chances, urge them, beg them, and show them how to be good employees. But we make it very, very clear that unless they participate with our program, we'll let them go.

Recycling is a beginning for us in job training. Ideally, I'd like to see us start a factory or packaging plant, where more people could be employed and trained in our philosophy. Employees would be required as part of their paid work week to attend SFBS classes on things like ethics, budgeting and parenting. Everyone would be involved, as all of us are in the other SFBS programs, in personal recycling – transforming ourselves into better human beings. Getting more disciplined, more sensitive to others, more aware, better educated. Whether volunteers or recipients, we're all into recycling – the business of transforming ourselves.

PHILIP STOAKLEY

WHEN PHILIP STOAKLEY WENT TO WORK IN SFBS' pilot recycling program in 1994, he had no idea that he'd wind up an avid watcher of a commodities market. The program that started with two couples, four churches and two vans now serves 38 businesses, nine churches and five schools. And the price of cardboard, aluminum, office paper and newspaper – driven by global market forces completely beyond Stoakley's control – determines whether on any given day he should sell or stockpile the materials he collects.

"When we first started, cardboard was going for $120 a ton – that's 2,000 pounds," Stoakley explains. "We're getting a lot more cardboard now, but the price dropped to $60 a ton, and in November, down to $30 a ton. Today, it's up to $85, so we're selling 120 bales that we've had to store."

"I still can't understand how the market can go from so good to so bad so quickly. It's somebody in an office somewhere that runs a plant and decides, 'We're not buying anything this month.'"

It's easy to see why so many recycling programs go out of business. Without the capital to invest in forklifts, balers, storage space and trucks, and without the financial cushion to weather price fluctuations, it is impossible to survive in the volatile business. SFBS's Recycling Program survives because it is filling a niche not previously served. It collects recyclables from small businesses, churches and schools that are too small to operate their own programs, and produce too little to entice major recycling companies to pick up their waste. Today, the program brings in about $3,000 worth of recyclables each month.

"We went from four churches to eight churches," Stoakley explains. "Then, people who went to the churches would say, 'Hey, I have this business, and I don't want to throw stuff away, can you pick it up?' " So Stoakley, a 36-year-old former Marine, and his crew of formerly homeless workers, set about their rounds to strip malls, lawyers' offices, travel agencies and property managers.

Everything they pick up is hand-sorted by workers earning at least $6 an hour.

Stoakley looks at the barrels of paper, empty soda bottles, discarded travel vouchers and computer paper and sees barrels full of nickels and dimes.

"People have a hard time seeing the stuff they throw away as actually being money they're throwing away," he says. "But that's what it is."

Before turning it into real nickels and dimes, SFBS collects 30,000 pounds of newsprint, 40,000 pounds of cardboard, 600 pounds of aluminum and 3,000 pounds of glass each month. All of it is material that would otherwise be tossed into a landfill.

Stoakley is a wiry, intense man who speaks rapid-fire and is constantly thinking of ways to streamline, expand, get better organized. "Why not have a poster contest for kids at

the schools involved in the program?" he wonders aloud. "The kids would learn about recycling in the process, and the winning poster design would be used to decorate the program's recycling barrels that year."

At the moment, however, Stoakley is consumed with moving the recycling program to an 11,000-square-foot warehouse at the abandoned Mather Air Force Base. The warehouse is being re-roofed, re-wired, sheetrocked and cleaned to house the program, now competing for space in the Oak Park Food Locker warehouse.

A grant from the State of California has just been awarded to the program – enough money to purchase a new cardboard baler and forklift. When the Mather warehouse

is completed, more employees will be hired from the base's homeless housing program.

In the Marines, Stoakley ran a dining program where he supervised 70 people, preparing meals for 800 people at a time.

"So I know how to get people to work," he says. "The hard part is, because of where most of my employees are coming from, instead of just getting on 'em and being hard about it, I have to look at it a little differently, and sometimes give them a second chance. I also have to babysit them, in a way. Many of them just never got the job skills down. They're used to just skating by. So if I don't show them just exactly what to do, they might do half of what they're supposed to do."

Stoakley, a perfectionist himself, used to spend weekends on his own time straightening up the recycling warehouse. Now he says he is learning not to let the imperfections inherent in the job "get on my nerves so much."

"You have to remember this program is about much more than the almighty dollar," he says. "We're giving guys a chance, and we're spreading the work of the Food Bank out in the community."

Often, Stoakley says, employees will ask why they should bother picking up recycling from a small business that really only has enough to pick up once a month. "The question is, how much more might that business do for the Food Bank? This is a way for people to get to know about us, even if we don't make money in picking up their recyclables. If we're in their face more than once a year at Christmas, maybe when they have something to donate, or want to remember a charity, they'll remember us."

Stoakley says he's proud how far the program has come, considering "we didn't have anyone tell us, 'Here's what you do.' "

"When Father Madigan first asked us to start this program, we had a semitrailer out in the parking lot, and that was all," Stoakley recalls. "He told me he started his Food Locker the same way and in 20 years, look how far that has come."

MATTHEW OSBURN

MATTHEW OSBURN, A LEAN, SIX-FOOT-FOUR, 36-year-old man, looks hard into your eyes for just seconds, then averts his eyes and faces away as he tells his story. It is a disconcerting mannerism until you hear his story, and imagine how the habit was formed. Osburn is foreman of the recycling crew, and one of Stoakley's most reliable, conscientious employees. His calloused, ebony hands testify to long hours of manual sorting and lifting, and he wears a recycling program cap proudly each day. He was born on a small farm outside Birmingham, Alabama, the seventh of nine children. Childhood, he says, "was an experience I wouldn't like to live again."

Growing up in racially segregated Alabama, he recalls when "blacks and whites weren't allowed to be together on any level, even to work together."

The family raised chickens and had a few cows. "We used to come into the city with our wagon, sell what we could of the milk, eggs and cheese that we made. Most of the time we got run out, 'cause, like I said, it was that kind of town. You weren't allowed to be mingling or mixing. Even in the '60s and the early '70s."

"I used to take it personally," Matthew says of the racism in the South. "It used to make me feel like I was a leper, and everyone else was like, straight. Now I can see it like it's their problem, and I don't let it bother me anymore.

"Oh, it's still there. I've been back for a visit. It's on a higher level, now. Whereas it used to be they'd walk by you and call you the 'N' word, now what they'll do, they'll just look. As if they're looking through you. You don't exist. And I'll smile, 'good mornin' and I'll keep going. I can't afford to let it affect me anymore."

When his family sold their farm and moved into Birmingham, Matthew left home and moved in with an older woman who treated him like her godson. He was 14 and stayed in school, but dropped out in the 11th grade when a football injury stole his glory as quarterback for the Parker High Thundering Herds and sent him into a deep depression. In 1976, Matthew got his GED, but was well on his way to becoming addicted to gambling. At 20, he decided to leave the South.

"I planned to go to New York," he recalls. "But my father said, 'Go to California.' He said the difference between California and New York was like being in the jungle with a bunch of hawks or being in the jungle with a bunch of lions. Now, you would think the lions would be stronger than the hawks. But the fact that the hawks can fly, see, he said, 'I suggest you go to California and deal with the lions.' He was telling me the train in New York was too fast for a country boy just first going into a big city. He figured I would've gotten eaten up alive."

He nearly did, but in California. "It was like first coming into a party where everybody there knows everybody and you don't know nobody," he recalls. "Not only did I not know my way around, I didn't know anything about the people, as far as the difference between the South and the West. In the South, even though you had your racism and your prejudice, you still had what you call your southern hospitality. And I found none of that here. I found people were cold, ruthless, some were even heartless. It was like, 'You take care of yours, I'll take care of mine.'"

He got a job as a construction worker, and one of his first paychecks was taken from him at gunpoint at a liquor store. He suspected a co-worker of setting up the robbery.

"It took me 18 years to be able to trust anybody as a friend. I had a relationship that lasted 8 years, and we were good to each other, but as far as trusting anybody outside of a relationship, no."

He worked construction jobs for two and-a-half years, and in 1982, he says, "I started back to my old pastime, gambling. You name it. Poker, craps, pool table, football, basketball, boxing. From '82 till '89, that was my only source of income. It sufficed. Wasn't a glorious life, but it kept my head above water."

Matthew lived in downtown Los Angeles, in a neighborhood he referred to as "the pits," 'cause everybody down there was some kinda dependent. It was either drugs or relationships, or alcohol. Everyone had something besides themselves that they needed to get through every day. For me, it was gambling. I can think of maybe three days out of those seven years that I didn't gamble. I was addicted to it. It was a way of life. It *was* my life."

When his 8-year relationship ended over his gambling and his girfriend's drug use, Matthew moved on, to Las Vegas. There, instead of succumbing to the craps tables, he fell in love and got married. He says his wife, Loretta, is "the backbone of me not wanting to gamble."

She encouraged him to get a nursing assistant's license and the couple worked in nursing homes awhile. They moved around the country, with Matthew doing farm labor, construction, factory work and convalescent home jobs. Finally, in 1992, they wound up in Sacramento, where Loretta's grown daughter lives.

"When we got here, about the first three or four months we were homeless. Just living from shelter to shelter," Matthew recalls. In between shelters, they lived on the banks of the Sacramento River. Then the couple was accepted into the Havens Transitional Housing program at SFBS, and "that's what really turned it around."

Having mentors, he said, was difficult at times. "My wife is a strong-willed person, Paula (the program director) is a strong-willed person, and they used to butt heads all the time over everything."

They agreed on one thing: Matthew needed help to get over his addiction to gambling.

"It was like a period in my life where I was deciding: did I want to go back to gambling, or did I want to have a life? I didn't know, until Paula and my wife made the decision for me, in July of 1994. Loretta told me, "You've got to make a choice: love me, and care for me, or you're gonna love gambling without me."

"That would wake anybody up. I mean you can love something you had a long, long time, then you find something you love more, and you ask yourself which one is the most important? Gambling couldn't hold a candle to my wife. I didn't want to lose her, under any circumstances."

At the same time, Paula found out about Matthew's gambling addiction and directed him to Gamblers Anonymous, a program he'd never heard about. He's been going ever since.

"That was July 13, 1994, and thank you, Jesus, to this day I haven't gambled. I go to meetings once a week, sometimes twice. It keeps you focused. It lets me know if I ever slip and go back to it, I'd be lost."

At SFBS, Matthew says, "I learned you get outta life what you put into it. This job has been good. Eighty percent of it, anyway. The 20 percent you don't like you're gonna get with any job."

That 20 percent frustration, in Matthew's case, is dealing with co-workers who aren't as enthusiastic or grateful about their work as he is. It gripes him, he says, when he sees someone not giving the job their all.

"That attitude comes from people believing the world, that society as a whole owes them something. I know that from personal experience. I've thought that way myself. Felt that I'd been cheated. Especially once I got out here from Alabama.

"Now I know you've got to look at it like, this job is what keeps me alive. It's my substance to live. If I can't give a little extra here and there, or sometimes a *lot* extra here and there, to surpass and to improve it, when the program dies, as most of the people here don't realize, we're out, too.

"There's no one center I've ever been in or heard of that strives to help as many people in as many ways as this place does. Gives you clothes, food, sometimes help with rent deposits, your light bill, gas bill. And to actually take somebody off the streets, and put them into a place, and allow them to pay 20 percent of their income to live in that place? I mean to restructure their life, whereas in a year, two years max they can go back out on their own, and really start their own life? I think that's grand. That is truly grand."

(Matthew asked that his real name not be used to protect his privacy)

Yia Chang's daughter visits SFBS

C O N C L U S I O N

"Nemo dat quod non habet" is a statement that has remained with me since my seminary days. It says: "You cannot give what you have not got."

Bishop Fulton Sheen challenges us even further when he says: "I would rather see a sermon than hear one."

And Will Rogers adds his piece by saying: "Know what you are doing. Love what you are doing. Believe in what you are doing."

All social service agencies love and believe what they do. But I wonder, are all social service agencies fully aware of what they are truly trying to accomplish?

I say this because experience has shown me that many poor people are perfectly content with just receiving catering help. And that many agencies seem fulfilled in merely rendering such a service.

However, I cannot help but feel that this approach accomplishes very little. Pauperization flourishes. Self-actualization stagnates. And self-esteem and ethical values are placed on the back burner.

I also question if government can ever teach moral values. And I question even further if agencies that rely heavily on government funding are rendered impotent by that very reliance.

This is the thinking that has motivated our operation over these past 20 years to bypass bureaucracy. To turn to church pews, civic organizations and humanitarian individuals for hands-on volunteer help. And at the same time to embrace the entire Sacramento populace for our needed financial support. Ninety-three percent of our funding comes from local donors, less than seven percent from government grants. Some people are in a position to give money, others are in a position to give of themselves. We've been extremely fortunate to have an advisory board of business and community

leaders who have done both. Over the last ten years, board members have personally donated $800,000 of their own money to keep our programs thriving.

Basic grass-roots organizing has worked well for SFBS. Rather than preoccupy ourselves with problems or bogging ourselves down with bureaucratic solutions, we've

industrial printing and cutting machines, we have folding, sorting and stapling equipment. Through our volunteers and donated equipment in the area of printing alone, we save hundreds of thousands of dollars.

Because we are virtually self-sufficient, we needn't fear that government cutbacks might threaten our existence. Each time we've tackled one need, another has become apparent, and we've seized the opportunity to develop new programs. Our aim is to lead our clients toward self-sufficiency. Unless we do this, I believe we will only be participants in their pauperization.

Our latest program, the SFBS Family Learning Center, is getting off the ground with that philosophy in mind. From our experiences with both the Mother-Baby Program and the Reading Center, we saw the need for a place where parents and their preschool-aged children could learn together. Immigrant parents learn English while their children receive instruction to prepare them for school, together in a homey, welcoming environment. In addition to weekday classes for parents and their toddlers, evening workshops in budgeting, parenting and family activities are offered. Parents are asked to make a commitment to this program, one that reflects their willingness to move themselves out of dependency.

In developing this latest program, we wasted little or no time with bureaucracy, nor did we wait for government grants to fulfill our visions. We had already gathered a volunteer advisory board to plan the pro-

chosen to focus on the multitudinous opportunities for doing good each day.

Our work could not be done without the energy and generosity of nearly 800 volunteers. I spend many hours acknowledging the generosity of our donors, personally signing notes to approximately 15,000 people each year.

All of our newsletters, brochures, flyers, notepads, Christmas cards, and special invitations — tens of thousands of pieces of paper each year — are printed in our own shop on donated press equipment, and designed by our one very capable printer, Clyde Rice. Paper is bought for cents on the dollar by the skid — in sheets the size of a pallet — then cut to size with an industrial-sized paper-cutter. In addition to our gram, when I was approached by Sister Jane Golden, a longtime educator in Sacramento's elementary and high school systems who also had several years' experience in bilingual education programs. She had no knowledge of our plans for a Family Learning Center, but stopped by one day to chat with me and find out what sort of educational component we had going at SFBS.

It dawned on me as we talked to ask Sister Jane if she would direct our new program. She accepted, then and there. It was one of the many serendipitous occurrences at SFBS that reminded me that Somebody bigger than ourselves is doing the planning.

That meeting was less than a year ago. The Family Learning Center is now thriving in a donated home next door to the Reading Center, with volunteer tutors, computers, toys and books. In the very near future, SFBS plans to allot Sr. Jane 6,000 square-feet of building for her operation.

In the Family Learning Center, as in the Reading Center and Mother-Baby Program workshops, we engage in a partnership with our clients, one in which they actively participate in the work necessary to achieve self-sufficiency. But how can we expect our clients to become self-sufficient unless we model self-sufficiency ourselves? By thriving as a volunteer and donations-based organization, I believe we provide a daily example of the philosophy we strive to impart.

POSTSCRIPT

Since the interviews for this book were completed, Akennya has married a man she met at church. The family is now living in their own home, and Akennya is one semester away from earning an Associate of Art's degree in criminal justice. Audrey continues her work with Don and was able to read the chapter about herself and the Reading Center. Philip Stoakley became a proud father. Joe Ostoja and the Sunday lunch gang still show up every week to slice Spam and cheese, foregoing TV sports.